The Poetry Review

The Poetry Society, 22 Betterton Street, London WC2H 9BX

The Poetry Review

The Poetry Society, 22 Betterton Street, London WC2H 9BX
Tel: +44 (0)20 7420 9880 • Fax: +44 (0)20 7240 4818
Email: poetryreview@poetrysociety.org.uk
poetrysociety.org.uk/thepoetryreview

Editors: Andre Bagoo and Richard Scott
Publishing Manager: Jane Ace
Administration: Astra Papachristodoulou

ISBN 978-1-911046-36-3 ISSN: 0032 2156
Cover: *Emerald Isles* © James Short 2022, www.jshort.art
Cover quote by Kevin Breathnach, see p. 47

© The Poetry Review & The Poetry Society, 2022

· · ·

SUBMISSIONS
We welcome submissions. Guidelines available
at poetrysociety.org.uk/thepoetryreview

ADVERTISING
To advertise in *The Poetry Review*, visit
poetrysociety.org.uk/thepoetryreview or
contact Ben Rogers on +44 (0)20 7420 9880,
email: marketing@poetrysociety.org.uk

BOOKSHOP DISTRIBUTION
Central Books, 50 Freshwater Road, London
RM8 1RX, UK. Tel: +44 (0)20 8525 8800
or visit centralbooks.com

PBS OFFER TO POETRY SOCIETY MEMBERS
The Poetry Book Society offers Poetry Society
Members a special 10% discount (plus postage)
on books bought from poetrybooks.co.uk.
Contact The Poetry Society: +44 (0)20 7420
9880 or membership@poetrysociety.org.uk

SUBSCRIPTIONS & SALES
Individuals UK: £38 / Europe: £48
Rest of the World: £53 (delivery by airmail)
Single issue: £9.50 plus postage.
Order online at poetrysociety.org.uk/shop

Subscribe to the digital archive of *The Poetry
Review* at exacteditions.com/thepoetryreview
The Poetry Review is on sale in leading
bookshops. It is also available on audio CD.

The Poetry Review is the magazine of
The Poetry Society and was first published in
1912. A subscription to *The Poetry Review* is
included as part of membership of The Poetry
Society. Views expressed in *The Poetry Review*
are not necessarily those of The Poetry Society;
those of individual contributors are not
necessarily those of the Editor.

Charity Commission No. 303334.

*The Forest Stewardship Council (FSC) promotes environmentally appropriate, socially beneficial,
and economically viable management of the world's forests. By buying products with an FSC label you
are supporting the growth of responsible forest management worldwide. The Poetry Review is printed
with vegetable-based inks. Surplus inks, plates and printing blankets are recycled.*

CONTENTS

Poems

Wilful Re-readings

Poems

Tributes

Reviews

EDITORIAL

There are ghosts in this issue. Our first conversations arose out of the centenaries that have already or are about to fall, not only of T.S. Eliot's *The Waste Land* but also Rainer Maria Rilke's *Duino Elegies*. Last year was also the birth centenary of the great Guyanese poet and novelist Wilson Harris, and August marks the birth centenary of Philip Larkin. But we didn't want simply to commemorate these moments; we wanted to push further. Extended critique soon turned to something more creative and queer. In the spirit of the late theorist Eve Kosofsky Sedgwick, whose queer readings revolutionised literary theory itself, we asked essayists to re-read these texts reparatively and wilfully with the hope of unearthing ultra-relevance, pleasure and distortion. Queer readings became Wilful Re-readings. But of course, we had no idea what to expect. We were stunned by the responses: Mark Wunderlich's psychogeographical project of searching for Rilke; Kevin Breathnach's dramatisation of how Eliot's fragmentary text might inspire and conjure the many fragments of a queer life lived through art and observation; Lara Pawson's consideration of how Larkin's poetry might be recalled and read post-Brexit; and Gemma Robinson's tracking of the fingerprints of Harris's poetics within his prose.

Such wilful re-reading has much to offer the poet too. And might there be some consolation, a wisdom, in other texts and voices? A poetic ancestor to be in dialogue with during these difficult, terrifying and even unrecognisable times? 'To wish to know everything Faust says you must become nothing', writes Sandeep Parmar in her poem sequence 'FAUST', which engages with Johann Wolfgang von Goethe's language and ideas. Can there be something beautiful in this nothing, this disappearing act, where found words or ideas take over? Are we not like the characters in Parmar's poem, 'girls in another century baring our arms in an inhabited garden'? The garden of poetry is already inhabited; we are not alone. The speaker in Peter Gizzi's poem 'Dissociadelic' similarly suggests we have 'crossed over into ink', fusing with language itself. This fusion reflects there being something both different and utterly familiar: 'inside the song' we find 'Blurs. Gestures. Something loved.' But rather than all this being a hopeless realisation, the poem urges: 'When you're brought to your knees, / sing a song of praise'. A cure for many things, including the speaker's dissociation, might just be the 'black shimmer' of text on a page. Perhaps this is the dance of many of the poems within these pages, something found and intertextual yet something unique and idiomatic. 'Far-fetched, // a line comes back / to meet itself' writes Rae Armantrout in her poem 'Proof' as if to illustrate this.

Other hauntings occur here too. 'If you endure at all, you do so transmuted and scattered', writes Fran Lock in her elegiac and celebratory tribute to Roddy Lumsden. Influence, and Lumsden's was vast, is a voice 'simultaneously summoned and distorted' proposes Lock. Maybe this intertextuality, this foundness, is a beneficent haunting of sorts: new work is always in conversation with what has come before. 'Death itself has lost', declares the late Iliassa Sequin in her 'Quintet 7'. Of course, death has not lost and we grapple with it in the world of poetry just as in the larger world, but we protest it with language, both found and fresh. In his long poem 'BESIDE   SEASONAL', J.H. Prynne sets about revivifying and skilfully 'ransack[ing]' the haunted, even derelict, structures of English itself writing a bestiary of sorts, teeming with 'bee-hives', 'reindeer' and 'white mice' with all their 'billow [and] burrow'. And in Carol Watts' topical sequence 'Ghost Ponds', the land's topography becomes an arena for resistance against oppression where 'inert & dormant seeds' might spring forth, bringing back life. Perhaps this, then, is the dance of the words in this issue – new life, a liveliness, stemming from ghosts. 'Lavender sprouts through the corpse', writes Breathnach in his response to Eliot; lilac and hyacinth bloom again, only refracted, queered.

Andre Bagoo and Richard Scott

NOELLE KOCOT

Peanut Butter

If I say, I didn't deeply
Suffer,

It would be a lie.
Look at that flower,

Blooming in the field
With grassy amazement.

See how those lumps
Of peanut butter

Disappear
Indifferent and even fragile

Down the ravenous
Mouth.

Corned Beef and Cabbage

What occurs. Something
Difficult

Far away.
Ideograms across the grass,

The slow boil
At six a.m.

Impossibility of the
Gorgeous,

An edible perfection
Of impermanence,

An illustration
Of transparence,

As if so much good fortune
Is feathers

In rainwater.

Out of Hiding

Lavish sky, utterance.
Though evidence

Suggests
I am singular,

I beg to differ.
How happy they seem

Over there!
Fulfilment of a watery

Sphere,
Life seems like lead

At times,
And the weight I carried

Was nearly frozen.
We lose ourselves

In iridescence.
The one soul is a cipher,

The other,
A future flame.

DANTE MICHEAUX

Abyss

The hole in the stage is a black hole
and – too – a kind of sexual ambition:
earlier, on some warm summer nights,
it was deadly, contagious but the trickle
of joy that sometimes fear can sustain
pulled and pulls still, the locked eyes
of a go-go boy through the smoke, whatever
risk, it will have you whether it desires
to or not, the physics of the universe
being not unlike addiction, you may
think you are cured but never really are.

CAROL WATTS

Ghost Ponds

What returns as a depression
in the ground, as if in a surfacing

of something not yet brought to mind
or recovered,

takes the form of a hand
in the black soil, Iryna's hand.

A germination of past burials,
ancient & apocryphal, shadows

this *grim season of planting &
replanting,*

contending brackishly with air,
invasive arrivals.

Revealed from the sky, levelling
industrial fields, violence

tills in time, forcing remembered
seasons lived in common

to evacuate their trouble, cached
in naturing of the same.

So storks gather again, spring ignites,
seeding its younger greener ghosts,

living between land & air, buoyed
up where surface tension is bent

on return. Say hope is a vegetal spectre,
a name for earth's meniscus.

Iryna isn't held there. Her nails are red,
manicured with a purple heart.

Care finds repositories in the naming of grief
this spring can't restore.

To find its own long return, nothing natural in it.
It was March 5, she was cycling home.

Time arrested. Words forego witnessing,
inert & dormant seeds

trapped by winter's cruelty, the way cold extracts
life from the ground, keeping it docile.

The screaming of ponds, so many silent
mouths.

Note:
Reference to a 'grim season of planting and replanting' is from the article 'This land is in blood: A Ukraine village digs up the dead', in the Economic Times India online, April 17 2022.

JAKKY BANKONG-OBI

ideograms for the hawk-moth and for the aftermath fire

i. dusk is something to wallow in.

ii. antlers on a hilltop, sunned and bifurcating.

iii. scry of crow on the withering branch.

iv. black shadows feathering secret rendezvous with home.

v. the gloaming, a masque headdress: relic of a time honoured ritual of
   uncovering.

vi. audience of crickets in the underbrush.

vii. *whatever sees us, sees us.*

viii. deep ancestral hour of night.

ix. a felled log.

x. brush of mushroom beside.

xi. longing unmakes.

xii. haunt of charcoal on ochre skin.

xiii. dancing *under the full moon.*

xiv. lightning strikes three times.

xv. a thousand fires kindle and rage.

xvi. lovers learn the shape of desire.

xvii. secret: body crumbles at the slightest touch.

xviii. a moth's chitinous wing.

xix. arcs you into open flame.

xx. blurring the lines of luminance and shatter.

in a year of flowers

in a year of flowers i confess, i cannot tell cirsium
from gardenias, in december's austere mien.
tropical and perennial, their scurried stalks
remind me: *despite air, the fallow field.*
                          the mud-caked river. long and drawn out
                          like winters of snowed-in-meadows, elsewhere.

still.
praise the resilience of aloes, the wild
pistillate of clerodendrum and ixoras
fingering the crusted and bare spine, dendritic
through harmattan's dolorous days. wait
                          until february thaws
                          grim-eyed nettles, rangy

jatropha and a scattering clematis from the waking
gyre; the world, a slow moving garden-reveal
april sings in the muted tones of frangipanis & morning
glories. all of it dewy with the sheen of first love.
                          that bated breath or the hum
                          before the kiss – is may,

a culled storm that breaks into june just right, it sets
everything blooming. lush and carpeting green moss
in cool meadows i could laze forever in
but the jacarandas' bunting. *what will be will be love's*
                          first blush as hectic as
                          a flush of hydrangeas in july,

roses and calla lilies rouging in their sultry mead: the humidity,
a fecund domain. what riot of moths and bees
will resist. to *nectar?* the honey and the honeycomb.

the fore-glow of august
as the quiet reckoning of linear time.

the harvest is a bouquet of posies, accents
of celosia and jasmine, lantana and queen-of-the-night.
tendrils of trade winds on the heels of a crisp october
rumours of distant storms we have weathered.
a climatic anticlimax we can tell this
time will be harder. to survive,

they will have to go back, to seed
hunker down. to bloom again.
root.

SELIMA HILL

The Visitor

My visitor is a handsome spider,
six foot tall and elegantly dressed,
who perches on the arm of my sofa
saying nothing, as a spider must.

Dawn

Half-asleep,
at dawn,
I see a spider
whose tiny face
is trying not to cry.

The Handsome Spider

I called the spider handsome
but he's not.
Which is fine.
I don't like handsome spiders.

Knees

He's like a spider made of eyes and knees.
Please don't be afraid to sit still.

The Little Beanie

So this is what it's like
to see a spider
in a little beanie
on my doorstep.

The Snail

I used to keep a snail in a tank,
a long glass fishtank, all along one wall.
I tried to give him everything he needed
and make his life as comfortable as possible.
The first thing I would do every morning
was see where he had got to in the night,
I'd peer into his little faceless face
and wonder where he came from and how old he was
and whether he could dream, or feel lonely,
and all the time I knew him and cared for him

he never complained; on the contrary,
he seemed quite happy in his glass home
and didn't seem to mind being watched,
or being offered curious fruits;
courteous and grateful, he would sit
beside his little rock for hours on end
as if to say, or chant, *who needs plans?*
It's true he wasn't cheerful exactly
but to me he was, and always will be,
sinless and beautiful, like you.

TIMOTHY LIU

Mystical Love Poem

I want to be the most
succulent bird

smaller than a fist

who flies right in
to your cast-iron pan

where the oil sizzles –

Bromance

When I left your place,
I tried to make my way inside

a tree. I didn't know where

to begin. I mean the thing
weighed over a ton and was

firmly rooted. I carried

something in my arms you'd
given me – was it still

breathing? Communicable?

Do I have to wait for another
ten years before you're willing

to meet again? The ground

under my feet felt very
soft. I wouldn't have been

surprised by treasure buried

underneath. I was hundreds
of miles from any coast

but could hear the bilge

of what I was pushing through
the storm right on up to my

inner left ear – waxy build up

only a child knows when folks
are sound asleep and has

no choice but to start digging –

MIGUEL MURPHY

Tarot

a cross, a crown, a spear
    – James Schuyler, 'Procession'

Like sex; the bewildering
thrill of winter flowers; and midnight at noon.
And the young girl that Christmas on the radio news
murdered by two sailors from a shipping liner.
George Michael, too, singing *My God*

I don't even think that I love you...
The invisible organist plays an anthem by Berlioz,
mindful, troubled. Countryside (untranslatable
sea, aching there) naked from the window;
I think of getting a new tattoo: anchor, dog, or rooster.
A wave. I don't even think that I love.

The view of the cathedral Hallgrímskirkja!
The underworldly hue.
Unnerving calm, a winter
bay of algal paste of blue, and the city pool
dark afternoons in Reykjavik.
The scalding outdoor tubs were lined with ice.

XIAO YUE SHAN

conjuring

there is no room left for disbelief, we have unsang
the songs. have stripped stones of magic. we gave
the gods power and took it back. our miracles lay
wrecked in roman columns, in the fragmented shapes
between starlight, their collapsible figures. enough proof
of faith. enough convalescence and abstract scripture,
evocations of hymn, oil-weight of paintings and their
surrendering strokes, the paths by which impossibilities
came seeking resemblance, enough ochre-rimmed
desert mirages. animal we named and battered in battles
of ordinary victory. fables retold to nothing. history
unguarded against the endless survey of capitals. we've
earned a long sleep. dreamed of its possible contours
when nearing the threshold, comfort we caught in traps,
we've given the day everything. the siege white and brave
as horizon. any morning in which we stood alongside
the words, *it has passed*. attempts at reading murmuration,
other inhuman languages, gave the inexplicable its own
holiness. distance and its hypnosis, gold and its melting
temperature, incantations waning with anise, cinnamon-
smell. milk-potions and apple-carvings and oracles –
we've eaten our fill. all this to ward off the oncoming.
all of it to ward off what was already with us, the world
a question desperately seeking its own annihilation.
look around, my love. all these wild answers we've
made, and not one among them have stayed with us
through the impossible pacings of a single, waking night.

the man I love ran off with everything except my poems

there was a thought hanging like a trick of light on the door
as if it could fall at any second. we knew if it fell
it would make a sound like water. the thought communicated
with its wayward tracings that it did not know to whom
it should return. the door was a fiction of the thought,
who had changed it from nothing to have something
to hang to. my hair is yellow in the fiction. then it is black
almost as fact. your hair is walnut in the photograph,
until fact throws a wild light upon it. doors are a fact
of their swinging, and water has noiseless ways of
entering the room. your eyes are what filled the doorway
to pieces. in a book about love gertrude stein
says that her portrait from picasso is the only reproduction
which is always I. I, I want to take I, back from I. from
your eye of doors which lead powerfully into silence,
and an illegible, animal approach of resemblance.
the immortality desire inflicts is the perpetual living-on
of somewhere other, just as a door can only ever be
open or closed, never neither. just as fictions come to live
side by side with fact, and hair greys sometimes in sleeping.
the days all rest around in halves like oranges,
I, and I, and I laying between them, looking almost
like anyone.

BONNIE HANCELL

imagine _ me

i imagine you glowing in your wife's lingerie
leg up on the table / one hand cocked
the other telling me how to fuck my life up
you had me at scalpel.
you had me at bitch.
i imagine the low-lit room where
you watch me sprawl through blood
where you listen to me beg
through headphones in case sandra
wakes up suddenly / i imagine your
coiled dick sadly flapping as you
type 'shit for me boi'
type 'puke on your dick'
    'blood makes the best lube'
i imagine a sunrise without you
and smoke dirty cigarettes on
the corner / where a row of
flowering dogwoods spit
white petals on the tarmac
and no
i won't give you my name.
and no
i don't love you.
and no
i can't feel
a fucking thing

CHRIS McCABE

The Doppelgänger

There is nothing more symmetrical than a Doppelgänger; not even his interior.
He sits facing inwards like a haunted mirror. A man who is nothing but vapour
has no cause to vape. 'My life has had twins' the Doppelgänger thinks,
'and my thoughts the crew of the Medusa'. The Doppelgänger learns from the
    snake,
lies down next to himself to measure himself for the eating.
'I sometimes feel I'm being watched,' he says, 'like two vats of pasteurised
milk teaching each other how to sour.' 'Or like two priests fighting over the
    same Bible.'
If there were two 'Deuteronomies' it might be okay, but there is only one flood
    and the Doppelgänger always fills twice: one side for the light,
the other for the absorption of light. He has a waterline through his corpus
like a badly orientated banknote. Sometimes he worries he's forged himself.
When the Doppelgänger gets into bed, he tells himself to make space;
when he dreams, he ricochets his monsters from the amygdala to the cortex.
This is how it feels to have twice as much of everything & be half as full as
    anyone.
The Doppelgänger looks through the hospital glass, at himself under the knife,
his organs glistening like a city of glycerine. He says, '*you're* doing okay, how
    about me?'

Cryptocurrencies

O Love for wanton cryptocurrencies I paved our way,
mining a million transactions like a tinker playing soldiers
with invisible lead. What seemed so real at first, dispersed –
leaving balls of dead bullion across our bed.

We mined & mined in dim unrealisation of our roles.
Told we were investing our power to unlock rare jewels,
we were but clerks, validating the status of a currency
that would not exist without the graft of lovers like us.

When we tried to cash it in... How fake are the stars?

RAE ARMANTROUT

Sides

They fight about
which sides
of the compartment
the heart and star
bandages
should be on
until one cries
for help.

*

In the beginning
chaos sloshed around
uneasily.

In the other beginning
was the word.

*

'This is the long side,
just so you know,'
one notes,

and it goes 'downhill'
from there,

goes 'south'
as we used to say

cruelly

Machine Learning

While the old poetry
confuses light

with leaves
and mixes leaves up

with clothing,
'layered just right',

the new poetry
will address questions

the next generation
of AI

might want answered.

What is the meaning of disquiet?

How does it differ
from anxiety

commotion?

Is an ion
a component?

Are components
companions?

What does it mean
to have the same root

in a dead
language?

Proof

To test an impression
by putting it in words?

*

Bubbles are round because
the air inside
is trying to get out
and the air outside
is trying to get in.

You'll notice

cells and galaxies
are spherical as well.

*

Far-fetched,

a line comes back
to meet itself –

vehement and
tenuous

HANNAH LOWE

Sinnerman

I cried, power, power (power, Lord)
  – Nina Simone

Of all her songs, this was the one he wanted,
over and over, all jumpy piano, her fingers
frenzying the keys. Not the songs I loved,
bluesy or full of sorrow – *My baby just cares*
for me. I wish I knew how it feels to be free.
He'd never heard of her (this may be untrue)
until we watched the documentary,
curled up on my sofa. Halfway through,

I went to bed, and he watched the rest alone
then woke me creeping down the hall, shifty
as a burglar. 3 a.m. when I checked my phone.
Probably he was running off to her. Not
Nina Simone. The other woman. No, not
the other woman. It turns out that was me.

JAMESON FITZPATRICK

Discursive Voice

A 'pants part', in opera, refers to a male role written for a female voice.

Please forgive the crudeness of the terms in which I've accepted to speak.

Also called a 'breeches' or 'trousers role'. I prefer 'pants part' because I am a poet, writing in English.

From the German 'Hosenrolle'.

Pants parts are most often written for mezzo-soprano or contralto vocal ranges.

The characters written as pants parts are most often teenage boys. Their high voices are meant to convey youth, though they need not be played by young women.

Der Rosenkavalier's Octavian, sung by a mezzo-soprano, is one of the operatic repertoire's most famous pants parts.

If I could choose, I'd be a contralto, as I don't know who I'd be if I weren't deep-voiced.

Though I wasn't once, when I was a boy soprano.

Though if I were a contralto, I couldn't play the Marschallin.

To be fair: even if I'd stayed a soprano, to play the Marschallin I would have to have had a still different life. An opera singer's.

When I sang most seriously I preferred smoking, and not practising.

I still do, though I smoke less and practise more now that I'm older.

In most stage versions of *Peter Pan*, the role of Peter is a kind of pants part.

He won't grow up.

Octavian, the audience must imagine, will.

When I was a child, I wanted to be anything but.

Hence the smoking.

Though my imagination stopped there, as though caught in the throat of something.

Wendy Darling Voice

The way Wendy knew was this:

One day, I was already old,

[...]

I was young until I wasn't.

I wasn't until I was young.

I wasn't, and I was young.

Until I wasn't I was.

Young, until I wasn't.

Young, and then I wasn't.

I was young until

I wasn't old, not yet,

but in a bad mood I might forget.

[...]

When I was young I was young before anything else.

I was young before anything.

I was young before.

After young came...

After young comes.

Wendy Darling Voice

Why did you go with him?

                         I had never been ravished.

Did you love him?

                         Of course I loved him.

As a child?

               When I was a child I loved as a child.

What did you do with his shadow?

       When I became a woman I put away childish things.

When did your childhood end?

                         When I loved him.

What ended your childhood?

                         That I loved him.

What did you become then?

                         A bird.

And you could fly?

                         He taught me.

And do you blame him?

             But you forget. He was a child, too.

Entre Nous Voice

Translating the Heroide, of course
I thought of you.
Her threat, your execution...

How can it be I'm older than you,
who was older than I was?
That you then would seem a young

man to me now. I took a detail
out from the poem
I wrote you: when you looked,

for a long while, out the window
at the place
you'd use to die. It felt

too transparent to be true,
too much,
as the truth sometimes is

and you often were,
are,
through the glass

through which I watch you, still
always
peeling your shirt at the party.

Entre Nous Voice

I hate the poem I wrote you.
Every time I read it I wonder if I should have kept the dash
where I replaced it with a comma, feeling,

as a good teacher once warned,
that my habitual overuse of dashes diminished their effect.
And also that, in that poem, where I put that comma, I didn't want

precision, but a sense of being provisional,
of thinking in real-time, though I in fact changed the dash back
and back again, over and over, until it was published.

I hate that comma. Just as,
in the next poem I wrote you,
I hate the word 'place'

for making me wonder if I should have said 'bridge'.
I hate the comma and the place
not because they're wrong, but because

I have to wonder if I was
when I re-read the poems, the first of which I do
not infrequently, because it is one that travels,

which is the reason I hate it,
because though it travels,
you do not live in it, or through.

It is less like a window than
a telescope, on the other side of which
you move further and further from me:

scintilla,
apostrophe,
speck-with-tail –

I saw that teacher recently, coming or going
from a classroom in the basement where I, too, teach.
I wanted to say hello, but didn't. So much has happened since.

LAURA ELLIOTT

Morning Alone

Eat the baby or else
all the fruits in order
like a machine.

Pineapple pineapple
cherry oops someone
just got in the way.

Girlish rootlet
sucking sparkling water
like it's vodka.

She's been still so long
the money spiders
sewed her arms together.

One idea then another
scraped clean
with the incisors.

Potter potter brain matter
sharpen the bread knives
open the bottles.

The wood pigeons don't remember
where in the bushes
they planned to settle.

There were roses
deep in their hoods
and lips burning in moonlight.

Marmalade indecision
and strangers walking
far too close to each other.

SAM RIVIERE

After Colours

As if to remind us that we're not quite alone,
there is a group of mysterious scientists who
seem willing to venture out into that unknown
realm, where nothing is entirely real. What they
find inside their minds is more complicated than
you may initially expect, or perhaps it is a form
you have long dreamt of discovering yourself...
Something to do with a hidden dimension and
the existence of strange creatures inside you.
For the time being, the secretists are keeping
this to themselves. In the new light of cosmic
awareness, they may be the first ones to realise
their visions of worlds that are almost beyond
description. For you, the reader of Inner Space,
the mysteries around you aren't yet revealed,
even though they have appeared for a few
seconds during my narration in this very room.
They exist now within you, as though they
always were there. Even today you are an
outsider in your own mind, an observer whose
existence is a reflection of that other presence,
like another star, or something trapped inside a
closed room, that forces it to manifest and
evolve in unpredictable ways – all without
ever revealing its inner nature.

Note:
This poem was composed using Generative Pre-trained Transformer 2 (GPT-2),
an open-source neural network created by OpenAI in February 2019.

KATY MACK

When the scarecrows come you must not question why

instead, let them in like an old friend
allow them to hang their ragamuffin coats
and sit at your table on the steadiest chairs.
Let them eat the decent bread
and drink the cider you'd been saving.
They may talk amongst themselves in the low hum
of telegraph wires on a hot summer's day,
they may swoop their pumpkin heads,
or unfasten their patchwork smiles,
but you mustn't read too much into it.
Affect an air of absolute self-assurance:
wear a casual blazer, unscrew the jar of pickled onions
like someone who owns many jars of pickled onions.
If one of them looks at you directly, look back
but not too intently; it has been said
that to stare into the eyes of a scarecrow
is like peering down the shafts of great wells,
some have been known to slip.
Of course, not everyone knows the way of scarecrows,
some can hear the click of the garden gate
free from the feeling that something inside
is unlatching. Imagine being such a person as this –
arranging tumblers along a kitchen shelf,
taking the small, clean weight of a whole glass in your hand,
turning each one against the light and simply thinking:
yes, this glass is empty, and yes, this one, empty also,
like someone who really believes it.

SANDEEP PARMAR

from *FAUST*

iv.

You ride the elevator to the eleventh floor of a hotel
      the tallest in our seaside town
            pale yellow or coral or white
                  no lighthouse but an abrasive plinth
                      chartered to the shore by cement.

Holy fathers, beatified men   their bronze or wooden statues dot
    the coast
        from San Diego to San Francisco
Up El Camino Real –
        where curved poles topped by soundless bells
                hang like sickles.

A river, a mission, a chapel, its garden.
        An ocean, a boardwalk, mountains, a freeway.
The town's Franciscan priest,
        Junípero Serra, once had his hands
doused with red paint. Genocidal
        churches, arable lands. A museum
with pieces of or whole Chumash
        bowls and other poorly-handled things.
School children appraise them. It is an annual ritual.

*

You request a room overlooking the Pacific.
The elevator does not stop; the hotel is never full.

A wooden pier – once of remarkable length –
    extends towards the Channel Islands,
draped in fog, reachable by boat
    if you wake with the fishermen before dawn.
A novel was set in those islands about the sole
    inhabitant of San Nicolas. The facts are:
a native woman alone for eighteen years
    spotted on the beach skinning a seal;
hauled ashore to the mission where dysentery
    killed her and her language off. She was given
a Christian name. We read it in school
    but remember nothing except
the word Aleutian and a numbness
    sharpened by no response. It was written
by a descendent of Sir Walter Scott.
    Scott was, among other things, an early translator
of Goethe. Dear sister. What you have learned is a dying craft.

The elevator opens onto a quiver of directions.

*

You drift back to a rose garden, a small women's college
    where each girl is permitted to pick and take
all the roses she can carry back to her room.

*

The pier, battered by storms, is rebuilt. A catafalque
      decked in American flags from sternum to navel.
From this angle, the sea is a parade of elbow length satin.
        Excavating the cave of the lone woman at San Nicolas,
diggers were halted by the Navy. It lies half-dug,
       disputed, full of sand, making distress calls.
You run towards the end of the pier with your arms
       open, lodging in its sights like a gale or target.

*

The room's ceiling is shot white powder,
      liable to yellow and stain.
Someone later recalled seeing you taking
      in the view from your balcony.
The sun is flattening into the sea and below
      there are families fishing or striding
in the dimming orange light. It is well-beyond
      happy hour in the tiki-themed bar,
the seafood restaurant we thought was so sophisticated.
      There's a revolving ballroom,
long since closed, where high schools held their proms.
      Corsages, rented limos, hairspray,
saliva drying on gums in windy sunroofs. The sun
      is a gold disc over the grey-blue waters of the Pacific.

*

To strive, you think, to know. You've brought with you a copy of *Faust*.
What is it to want to know everything. The light sharpens to a point
to a full stop to an ingot of gold at 7.30 p.m. This alchemy. Do you
open *Faust*. Do you leave it in the dingy room, on the beige bedspread,
a wager of its own in our Eden this Arcadia. Faust's strip of coastline,
a paradise built in his dotage, unbegun but in his imagination, an
inner light. Now you remember everything. You are in a state of sudden
alertness. You find your aim you strive. There is the sun, blinding all the

summer day. There is the cliff, where Euphorion dropped into blackness marching heroic. You think of the roses and how you carried them all in your arms. Striding full of hope into another century. To want, to owe, to feel shame. Dear sister. To wish to know everything Faust says you must become nothing Mephistopheles says to extend beyond what is human you must become the Spirit of Eternal Negation Faust says you must be willing to die but I am not afraid to die Mephistopheles says I will route your indentured soul from an eye an ear a navel a fingernail for the jaws of hell are always open Faust love has waded through my many dreams and orchestrations Mephistopheles opines we were all girls in another century baring our arms in an inhabited garden Care slips through the keyhole like smoke a kind of being without a kind of alchemy Faust you will never fall where love can be seen from a great height rising above these hills like a memorable star.

WILFUL RE-READINGS

On centenaries relating to Rainer Maria Rilke, T.S. Eliot,
Wilson Harris and Philip Larkin

...

Mark Wunderlich
Journey to Duino

This past August, when the curtain of the global pandemic
seemed to draw back for a time, I left my home in Upstate New
York and flew across the Atlantic in pursuit of a ghost. My pilgrimage
was one of several I would take as I set out to see the places Rainer
Maria Rilke had lived and worked. For some time now, I wanted to
see if by walking the streets of Prague, or wandering the parapets
of Duino Castle, I could glimpse some part of the world Rilke had
occupied. Would any of this help me better understand his poems?
I wanted to find out. In recent years I have bicycled along the little
canals cut through the marshy fields near Worpswede, Germany,
where Rilke lived for a time as a young man among a group of artists
building a community on the edges of the Teufelsmoor – the Devil's
Moor. I marvelled at the many fancy little dresses once worn by the
Infant Jesus of Prague, that little idol venerated as miraculous in a
church Rilke went to during his Bohemian childhood. I attended
the marionette theatre one wet afternoon in Vienna where I thought
about Rilke's essay on dolls, in which he pondered on the power
of objects to absorb the life around them. (After a performance of
Hansel and Gretel, during which the audience of children howled
at the appearance of the witch, we were invited to see the utter
strangeness of the scene backstage, with characters that had seemed
life-sized now dangled limply from strings in a half-sized world
meant to remain unseen.) So it was in August I found myself in Room
15 of the Palazzo Salis Hotel in Soglio, Switzerland, (formerly called

rather oddly the Pension Willy) high in the Swiss Alps, lying in a bed
which Rilke had slept in for most of August and September of 1919.
'Everything is just as it was when he was here,' the innkeeper told me
in her Italian-accented German, 'though the mattress is new.'

Soglio lies in the southeast corner of Switzerland high in the
Alps, and here Rilke resided for a period of a few weeks. In the many
settings for his cosmopolitan and peripatetic life, Soglio was but a
minor interlude. Clinging to a steep slope, the tiny village of about
150 inhabitants is surrounded by dramatic, snowy peaks. Walkways
wind past rustic stone houses and barns, little pocket gardens with
their mixture of vegetables, vines and flowers, and the cattle and sheep
in their stalls awaiting to be driven to mountain pastures. Soglio is
remote, picturesque, a point of departure for hikers and mountaineers,
though not particularly 'touristik', as the Germans say. The one little
tourist shop sells yarn from mountain sheep, honey, chestnuts, cheese.
The mountains all around are wild, imposing, shagged with dark pines.
Rilke didn't care for them, called them 'stupid', and to him the green
alpine meadows were nothing but a banal tourist attraction – though
there were few tourists to speak of then or now. Instead of gazing at the
majestic scenery, he turned inward, to the pretty formal garden behind
the hotel, with its boxwood hedges, its roses, the marble table he liked.
Here at the Palazzo Salis, he was given access to the library where he
would recline on a sofa, like the figurehead of a ship, and read. He
liked the smell of mouldering books, the chalky plaster walls, the old
furnishings that had been there as long as anyone could remember, and
which were imbued with just-hidden meaning, with spirit, and whose
connection to the past Rilke craved and fed upon.

In 1919, Rilke had been declared stateless, a citizen of nowhere and
everywhere. The world he had been born into and lived in – imperial,
polyglot, cosmopolitan – had imploded, and Rilke was in retreat,
yearning for solitude and desperate to take up once again the project
he saw as his great work, the *Duino Elegies*, which he had begun before
the war while on a stay in Duino Castle near Trieste, the Capitol of
Nowhere, as Jan Morris would famously call it, and which had been
bombed by the Italians to whom it now belonged. He had written at
least two of the elegies by 1919, and he had numerous fragments, but
the work had been set aside while he was drafted into service by the

Austrian army and set to work in the office of propaganda before being demoted to a basement file room – a job he both botched and despised. He was eventually discharged to what one imagines was the mutual relief of all involved.

My days and nights at the Palazzo Salis were spent contemplating Rilke's time there, and in my bag I had my own copy of the *Elegies* – a slim blue volume in German in its first American edition. I sat with it at the small, spindle-legged table where Rilke once sat, and I read from the poems he had written by 1919 and those he was yet to write in the coming months. I wonder if he had these drafts with him as he travelled here to this remote alpine spot, if he revisited the fragments he had begun years ago by the sea, when Duino Castle was the place of summer parties and visits from Archduke Franz Ferdinand where Rilke could retreat into solitude or where he was called on to pen the protocols during seances conducted in the Red Salon by his hostess the Princess Marie von Thurn-und-Taxis Hohenlohe and her son, a practising clairvoyant.

In a letter to his friend Annette Kolb written in 1912, Rilke wrote about the first elegy, 'I have no window on human beings. They give themselves to me only insofar as they make themselves heard within me', and of course I think of Rilke seated at a table, pen in hand, waiting as the medium's hand followed the planchette across a board and 'spoke' from behind a supernatural veil.

'The First Elegy' begins conditionally, describes the intrusion of the supernatural, a spiritual crisis, the poet crying out somewhere on a cliff above the Adriatic, the castle in which he was a temporary but recurring guest looming in the background. In the castle, the poet translated Dante, sat at Liszt's piano which he could not play (he claimed that he did not really understand music), ate his small vegetarian meals. Before arriving in Duino, he had been to Spain, and there he began to see Christianity as a 'fruit that has been sucked dry', and as a brew made 'with the same shreds of tea that have steeped now for two millennia'. In Spain he wrote that he saw Mohammed as being 'like a stream through a primeval mountain' breaking through to the one true God. We can see 'The First Elegy' as a private revelation received and recorded, at once grammatically obscure and emotionally fraught, a testament of great loneliness. The laces of syntax loosely bind up the poem which was born from his solitude – alone for hours in the castle, and a near madness, 'screaming like a wild man and clapping my hands' as he wrote to the Princess Marie von Thurn-und-Taxis Hohenlohe. This poem announces the arrival of a major work of German language literature, and its deep mystery and emotional charge explain the poem's enduring appeal – it has been translated by the likes of Vita and Edward Sackville-West, whose blank verse rendering has been this year re-issued by Pushkin Press in London to commemorate the poem's centenary. (The centenary of another major Rilke work, *Sonnets to Orpheus*, will be observed next year.)

I think of all of this work as I sit at a little marble table in the formal garden where Rilke sat, and again when I lie down in the bed he slept in, its wood frame creaking as I turn at night, the moon shining onto the stone roofs of the houses I see out the bottle-glass windows. On the wall of the room is Rilke's bill from the Pension Willy – framed now for posterity – and which he had signed, a pedestrian reminder of the care others took on his behalf, but which he paid for. I too take my meals in the dining room (Rilke liked its arched ceiling), and each evening of my stay, after having a drink on the front steps of the hotel, a young woman arrives to say, Herr Professor, your table is ready, and I go in to eat another solitary meal.

While in Soglio, I am alone with my thoughts, my notebook and my books, writing postcards to friends, living partly in the past as time collapses around me. I walk up the mountain slopes around the village under the canopies of chestnut trees, and I think I see simultaneously how much and how little has changed since he was here, almost a century before my own arrival in Switzerland. It's unclear if Rilke wrote anything significant while in Soglio; if he did, it isn't recorded. We do know that a great deal of correspondence had made its way to the hotel prior to his arrival, so I imagine him there mostly writing replies. When he left, he made his way to Zurich where he embarked on what would be a reading tour of German-speaking Switzerland. It had been ten years since he'd appeared in public, and over six hundred people turned out to hear him read. All accounts describe him as a captivating performer – charming and with a rich baritone voice, he had excellent patter and social instincts, flattered his audiences just enough.

It was in Switzerland that the *Duino Elegies* were reborn. From the fragments he had written years before in a castle that was now partly destroyed, he began to reconstruct and invent. The voice of these poems sounds as though spoken from the other side of human experience, as if the speaker had particular knowledge of what it was to be resurrected but who was haunted by what the interregnum had forced him to see and know. Begun in 1911 and published exactly a century ago in 1922, the *Elegies* have a world war inside of them. Their many leaps and disjunctures, their voices and stories pulled up from the past echo the clairvoyant's planchette tripping and reversing along a lettered board with the poet acting as medium.

I would leave Soglio the way Rilke arrived – with the Swiss Post. He arrived on the post wagon pulled by a single horse and wrapped in a borrowed fur coat, while I would board the bright yellow Post bus that would take me down the mountain first to Sils Maria (a town once famously occupied by Friedrich Nietzsche) then to a train heading to Zurich. My journey to Soglio showed me the fine line between solitude and loneliness. In 1919, Rilke was a refugee, the country of his birth had disappeared, and he worried about the expiration of his temporary visa, his homelessness, the devaluation of his meagre savings.

The great power of poetry is the way it moves us backward and forward in time, how it makes the dead speak, how when we read poetry from the past, it uses us – the living – as an instrument to amplify and revivify. In Soglio, I caught a glimpse of the lost world Rilke once occupied – I touched the furniture he touched, sat in rooms he ate and slept in. I walked the paths of the garden he so admired, leafed through books he may have read or borrowed, so perhaps that world is not as lost as it might seem? I don't know that any of this helped me to better understand his poems, but there are paths that lead to understanding that aren't about the intellect. Just as Rilke once looked at dolls, such as the marionettes I saw in Vienna, and asked whether such inanimate objects could attach themselves to the immaterial world, the insight I achieved was a tactile one that reinforced the power of poetry to make our world understandable.

Kevin Breathnach
A Handful of Dust
after T.S. Eliot

... ombre vane, fuor che ne l'aspetto!
   – Dante Alighieri

Carouselling so intense sleep paralysis is near, a snapped cotton bud in a drain by the door, a circular stain on the ledge in a foyer, apparitions in grammatical liaisons, elastic bands everywhere curled on the street, a page torn out of a book found under a tree, the snaking of oboes that score your immobile durations, the looping and phasing in Julius E's *Femenine*, reference to V, reference to K, some pages you open at random in G, the vertical shriek of a deer, the glimmer of a priest come late for the last rites seen through a sitting-room window, a handsome bed of hyacinths less one, recurrence of a number that I lived in, mirrors laid flat on the floor of A's *Tabula Ruža*, eyes with a frame in the passenger seat, stilettos drawn onto the legs of a table, pistachio shells in the garden, a scooter in front of a stretched limousine, marks on the spine of a copy of Clarice L's *Stories*, the frame of a window removed from its hinges, Medusa observed from a balcony blue through the morning, an earring that looks like an eyeball, typos in emails from very close friends, typos in emails from colleagues, a table beside you reserved for 6.30 by V, abstractions recalling *Im Gewitter der Rosen* by B, a child found dead in a field, a line out of C's *Peggy Sue*, receipt for some postcards you bought months ago between ominous parts of your journal, one or two lines about eggs, a woman laid out on the floor of a church on an island, a newspaper clipping gone yellow with age between pages of Jean G's *Le Balcon*, a hauntingly beautiful note of condolence you've not had the guts to reply to, errors in Google translations, corrections suggested for 'where', the fire alarm shrieking through half of her funeral, recurrence of a number that I lived in, the legs in A's sketch of her process, the motif surrounding V's head, vibrations of the door to the room where he lay on its hinges, the gardener parked at the top of the hill, the blades of the windmills you tilt at, conduction of light between objects in A's *Eight Times Folded*, the pattern of scabbing from scratches you do not remember, receipts from the bar in the hotel where R was found dead, the last rites delivered in line with restrictions, a mark in the eye on the sleeve of a book about G, a photo you send him of keys, gloves in the bar with carambola tables, a jocular handshake you share, a crude letter 'J' carved into a canvas, your psyche compared to the underground labyrinth in K, a triangle carved in the bark of the branch of a tree where you preach to the birds, confusion (as the priest pokes his head round the door) of relatives nearly bereaved, judgement discerned in the sound of inanimate objects, a name and address on a postcard of *Angst* by a man who it's said couldn't scream, the sighing of shelves standing over your shoulder, a fish in the hands of the man with a hand that you thought was a photo of yours, a knock from inside of your wardrobe, a coin on the floor when they leave, the rattling syntax of rain slowly dying, recurrence of a number that I lived in, reappearance of pens you thought lost on the shelf of your grandmother's medicine cabinet, the name of one radical theatre company, the order of letters in Messenger call URLs, invitations to parties you wish you'd left early, the shedding of petals through holes in a pocket, a black plastic bag in the back of a fridge that A tells you he wants you to see, tulips and snakes in the work of Ulrica H.V., the cancellation of a lecture on Tiresias, the priest looking nothing like the glimmer you'd seen, the cover of *The Joke* by Milan K, recurrence of a number that I lived in, unfamiliar tissues in your toilet at three in the morning, the song of the eyes in the mouth of the man with a dog near the Alte Pinakothek, a shape faintly traced in the space at the top of a print that J gave as a gift, visions that come as you stretch out the knots in your shoulder, unabated coughing by the fish-tank in a hospital reception, the anamorphic shadow of a willow, the scarf of an audience member, thick streaks of spit dried into the mirror in a house in which only you live, the strange double-folds in your copy of *Die Niemandrose*, the loops of a tractor reversing at speed round an obelisk built to remember, a coat worn down to a notion, recurrence of a number that I lived in, A's reference to *Under the Skin* in her early exchanges with me, a railing that looks like a 'W', a pencil A left on my desk when he called in one night for a drink, transparence and shells as motifs in *2together* by E, a statue with two heads divinely coupled in the crepuscule, the meaning of Milan and Jelena, a number underneath an illustration of a plover on the wall, the first fifteen minutes of *Lucky with A in Berlin*, a man rubbing crumbs from his thighs on the train while you read of a figure asleep on K's thigh in *The Castle*, an image of H on a muted TV as it loops old Liverpool highlights, reference to 'Inferno' on the front-page of a tabloid newspaper, a book I was given in an alley in Palermo on the subject of an elephant's bad dream, the right side-casing of a door along the left of your image, a Bulbasaur sprayed on the wall of the shelters, multi-sign adverts for oatmilk, a crack in the glass of the door to the house that my aunt quickly blames on the wind, a message discerned from the sound of the name of each letter on the spine of a book about *The Theatre and Its Double*, a clothes-hanger found on the street, the retrospective vertigo of magic first encounters, a glint in his eye listing writers who've died by their hand, the order of words in the title of games lined up on the shelf in the bar where you wait for a drink, a train setting off not the way you expected, the thrum of tall flags in the wind advertising a retrospective show of R's portraits, a trip to Lost Property days after B points it out, glamour emanating from the room beyond the room in which I sit, the image of Medusa on the shirt of a man cracking open pistachio shells, the stranger who asks if you are who I am as I tremble in front of a painting, certain books near to *Extinction*, uproarious laughter that follows a joke I hear end with the word 'shadow-self', an amulet worn as an earring, a spectral director that keeps you from sleeping one night when you stay in my room, the nonchalant grandeur of the venue, a hyacinth's decay, the pebbledash ruin of the venue, in the lining, the understated beauty of the woman who's working the door, of my coat, reference to 'skulls' by the men on the door whom you don't dare observe at all closely, a book left out on the table, recurrence of a number that you lived in, a canvas rehung upside-down, a film of the phoenix being carved out of sand played over the Angelus bells, 'B' in quotation marks neatly graffitied wherever you happen to wander, late-night sightings of an oversized chessboard in the clutch of a man like a shield, the fact you can't read what's revealed in *Atti relativi*, lavender sprouts through the corpse of a golden retriever, the arthritic plea of a glove in the grip of a branch yet leafless as you fall back in the unreal

Gemma Robinson
The Seasons of Wilson Harris

It took Wilson Harris two poetry pamphlets, a self-published poetry collection, numerous essays, an unperformed play, and at least three discarded novels before he felt he had found his creative voice. Working as a surveyor in Guyana (then British Guiana) in the 1940s and 1950s, his route to becoming a writer was not obvious. When he died four years ago at the age of 96, his name had become synonymous with a visionary artistry that is dazzlingly, even bewilderingly, cross-cultural. His twenty-four novels (all published by Faber from 1960 to 2006) pose an extended challenge to the limits of narrative realism and, as he would put it in the essay 'The Writer and Society', are an attempt to write fiction as a 'drama of consciousness shared by animate/ inanimate features'.[1] Starting with *Palace of the Peacock*, Harris, whose centenary was observed last year, honed a genre-defying language that experiments with myths and histories to reveal how 'apparently eclipsed voices and cultures' can re-emerge with renewed relevance for the past, present and future.[2]

It is tempting to frame Harris as a singular voice. However, he was part of a post-war generation of Guyanese writers, artists and political activists (including Jan Carew, Martin Carter, Eric and Jessica Huntley, Cheddi and Janet Jagan, Eusi Kwayana, Aubrey Williams, Denis Williams) who in their different ways were seeking to radically question the colonial world they had inherited. Like Harris, some were civil servants working in realms that encouraged them to rethink the freedoms they had as members of urban Guyana, and the duties they held to their fellow inhabitants and environment. For a time in the 1940s and early 1950s these differing interests intersected and ran in parallel. For example, the painter, Aubrey Williams, was an Agricultural Field Officer on the Guyanese coast. Here his support for exploited workers within British-owned sugar plantations resulted in a forced move to Hosororo in the north-western rainforest where he first encountered the Amerindian iconographies that would underpin his abstract painting. Martin Carter, a poet and founder member of the anti-colonial People's Progressive Party (PPP), worked in and then resigned from the prison service, forging a poetic vocabulary from these clashing experiences of liberatory political activism and incarceration.

Harris's work as a government surveyor meant often living within a crew navigating the serpentine rivers that weave Guyana into a South American hinterland as well as the Atlantic world of the Caribbean. This life encouraged him to imagine how humans might interact with the natural, geological, hydrological and astronomical formations that existed below and beyond the enforced boundaries of European global expansion. Although not a member of the PPP, Harris crossed paths with its members. He was good friends with Carter, and joined Georgetown discussion groups when he was not working in the interior. Eusi Kwayana, another founder member of the PPP, recalls Harris as a quiet listener. He remembers the group speaking about problems of class and society and then Harris's response being voiced in an 'entirely different idiom'. In Kwayana's words: 'the same class forces we were talking about he would call "the anonymous forces that were coming forward".'[3] We can get a further sense of this idiom by looking at Harris's comments on his first two poetry pamphlets. In a 1952 letter he attempted to explain the coherence of his vision to A. J. Seymour, the editor of the Guyanese cultural journal, *Kyk-Over-Al*: 'In *Fetish* I was concerned with the fact that the structures of civilisation man has built have become oppressive, since it has not been built in true accord with the energies or creative forms at its roots. Those sources therefore are bound to establish a distorted connection – sardonic, violent, protesting'. There are affinities with anti-colonial action here, but Harris rejects anything 'sardonic, violent, protesting' as energies too determined by oppression. He wanted something more but articulating that would not be straightforward.

He continues in the letter: 'After *Fetish* the ground has been cleared for me in *Eternity to Season* to meet the problem of a new world certain of the raw material of energy (psychological and creative) with which to build a structure truer to man'.[4] If his vocabulary of 'man' and 'civilisation' suggests that he is less sensitive to other 'distorted connections', like that of gendered language and its oppressions, his gravitation towards a register of 'energies' and 'forces' shows an openness to radically transformed modes of power and existence. I think it helped that Harris was born in the so-called 'New World'.

An anachronistic term for a colonial vision of the Americas becomes something else in his imagination: a chance to conceive the renascent parameters of exploited and exploiting communities, their limits and their freedoms. It was a lot to ask of a three-poem pamphlet. But Harris was pulling the idea of a new world in multiple directions to reimagine people and place.

The poems in the 1952 pamphlet *Eternity to Season* are ambitiously titled 'Troy', 'Behring Straits' and 'Amazon', suggesting that 'the problem of a new world' required a style informed by a mythic, social and environmental geography. It would encompass Greek myth and the fall of civilisations, as well as prehistoric patterns of migration, such as those that brought animals, plants and humans across the Bering land bridge (Harris uses the nineteenth-century spelling). In the final poem the Amazon is 'the world-creating jungle' that 'travels eternity to season' and its dimensions are multiple: it is river, falls, region, tide, 'living movement', 'the paradoxical stream' and 'green islands of the world'. The poem's imagery creates an imaginative geography where we are encouraged to examine and minimise our sense of human action: 'Branches against the sky smuggle to heaven the extreme beauty / of the world'.[5] Harris removes the human eye, and the depth range is aligned to that of tree and beyond. 'Smuggle' suggests transgression and secrecy, but the agency of the branches to communicate beauty is only illicit within a world already distorted by oppressive human structures. Much later, in conversation with Michael Gilkes, Harris expressed the kind of 'energies' or 'creative forms' he was interested in: 'language has to bring all the connections in if one is to find the beginnings of some kind of reverence for what we are, for the world in which we live, for a world that is endangered. And yet a world that is mysteriously potent and alive'.[6]

It is worth pausing on the phrase 'eternity to season' in relation to the idea of a revered but endangered world. As we read from 'Troy' to 'Amazon' there is an invitation to see ourselves within a connected mythology and ecology travelling away from the dangers of destroyed human Troy and towards the revered living Amazon. But such linearity does not fit with Harris's aesthetics of paradox and what he calls 'the unfinished genesis of the Imagination'.[7] The opening stanza of 'Troy' introduces the idea of 'eternity to season':

The working muses nourish Hector
hero of time: small roots move
greener leaves to fathom the earth.
This is the controversial tree of time
beneath whose warring branches
the sparks of history fall. So eternity to season,
the barbaric conflict of man.

These lines are taken from a third version of the poem. Harris worked on the phrase 'eternity to season' multiple times – as the title of the three-poem pamphlet, of an extended 1954 collection and a revised 1978 collection that Harris was invited to publish by New Beacon, the publishers and bookshop run by John La Rose and Sarah White. Read within 'Troy', 'eternity to season' starts to suggest danger and failure. Harris surrounds the phrase/title with two further phrases about history and conflict, and meaning is balanced ambiguously on the conjunction 'so'. Cast against the language of 'Troy', the word 'season' continues to evoke a cycle of natural change ('small roots move') and with it the idea of life and death. But following Harris's logic of energies, 'season' can also be distorted, to become a deadly time of 'barbaric conflict'. This differing meaning is held in tension across the poems so that when we read of the 'world-creating jungle' in 'Amazon', we cannot forget the potential dangers of Troy's 'warring branches'.

Harris's new world experiments extend into reimagining humanised landscapes and here also is a world in tension. In the expanded collections, we find poems that are sited in Guyana (in the village of Cumberland, settlements on the River Canje). They are places that the Martinican theorist Edouard Glissant might call 'points of entanglement'.[8] Forty years before Derek Walcott's *Omeros*, Harris looked to the Caribbean everyday and saw the possibility of a new set of global connections to make paradoxical sense of the complex histories of the region. Troy and Hector are creolised, activated not just by a fixed knowledge of Homer, but by the 'working muses' who in fathoming the earth should also acknowledge that 'Hector' was a name enforced upon enslaved men working on colonial plantations. In 'Cumberland', 'Ulysses' visits a cast of characters (Tiresias, Heracles, Anticleia), but they soon seem less bound to European mythology when you know that Cumberland faces the village of Ithaca across the banks of the Berbice river. Reading these lives within the frame of 'eternity to season' challenges our sense of time, and Harris invites us to read Hector's earth through the entangled frames of timelessness, and a decolonising timeliness.

To be of the 'new world' implies a relationship to the 'old'. Stuart Hall writes 'as a colonised subject, I was inserted into history (or in this case History) by negation, backwards and upside down – like all Caribbean peoples, dispossessed and disinherited from a past which was never properly ours.'[9] Harris's work faces 'the sparks of history' and unflinchingly sees 'barbaric conflict' through the expanded myth of Troy, and yet his language proposes other ways of seeing. In Harris's poetics, understanding negation, looking backwards and upside down feel like the routes out of disinheritance and dispossession. For Harris, a way through the cultural entanglements of the colonised world is to embrace a language that seeks to bring 'all the connections in'. By the time of his breakthrough novel, *Palace of the Peacock* (1960), Harris had worked hard to articulate a profoundly entangled world. If his poetry sought to bridge the extra-human and the human, to see the dangers of 'distorted connection' and oppression, and build a language that could help us see and hear the earth in all its multiplicity, his novels continued this ambition, creating a condensed figurative language.

In his first novel the unnamed narrator known only as 'Dreamer' moves from conquistadorial map-reader to reading the 'living landscape':

I pored over the map of the sun my brother had given to me. The river of the savannahs wound its way far into the distance until it had forgotten the open land. The dense dreaming jungle and forest emerged. Mariella dwelt above the falls in the forest. I saw the rocks bristling in the legend of the river. On all sides the falling water boiled and hissed and roared. The rocks in the tide flashed their presentiment in the sun, everlasting courage and the other obscure spirits of creation. One's mind was a chaos of sensation, even pleasure, faced by imminent mortal danger. A white fury and foam churned and raced on the black tide that grew golden every now and then like the crystal memory of sugar.[10]

Voicing the environment, Harris presents the potential for human consciousness to be in communion with animate and inanimate nature. Here it happens in extremity as the crew attempts to navigate a section of rapids, and the narrator grasps the once obscured limits of his world. Rivers are seen to tell their own stories. Rocks tell of the future, recalling 'timehri' rock carvings, an Arawak word for 'the mark of the hand' and signs of animist belief in Guyanese rivers. Golden reflections in the foaming, boiling water make themselves visible as 'the crystal memory of sugar' – a metaphor that glancingly returns us to the plantation histories of the region so that the words both hold on to and are liberated from their colonial connotations of violence, politics and commerce. The crew's journey (ostensibly a search for Mariella, the name of an Amerindian mission and an Amerindian woman) reperforms a series of traumatic pasts seeking a different kind of outcome. At the end of the novel, the 'dreaming' jungle reasserts its agency, Mariella eludes the acquisitive obsessions of Donne, the crew's Kurtz-like Captain, and all gather in the 'Palace of the Peacock', a place that is both waterfall and 'universe'.

As Harris's Guyanese multi-ethnic boat crew (now paradoxically both living and dead) reach the end of their journey they realise that '[e]ach of us now held at last in his arms what he had been for ever seeking and what he had eternally possessed'. The synthesising transformation that Harris seeks here – occasioning both self and community – is voiced as a collective belonging to 'one muse and one undying soul'. But if this singular eternal perspective is to make any sense, the muse must be seen as incorporating and caring for all the earth's seasons of experience, that is, in *Palace of the Peacock* the material cycles of pre-colonial and colonial exploitation cannot truly disappear but must be constantly reckoned with. This is the vital component in any attempt to understand how societies can transform themselves and transcend their divisions and alienation.

Over his long career Harris would absorb a set of vocabularies to elaborate his creative practice, from archaeology, music, history, to quantum physics, cosmology, geology and Jungian psycho-analysis. His novels would occupy multiple imaginative geographies within Guyana, England, Scotland, Mexico and beyond. His essays would become touchstones for critical communities seeking to understand postcolonial cultures and the demands of decolonising minds and institutions. In his note to *The Guyana Quartet*, a reissue of his first four novels, Harris writes about his work as 'a fiction that seeks to consume its own biases through many resurrections of paradoxical imagination and to generate foundations of care within the vessel of place'.[11] Harris published the pamphlet of *Eternity to Season* as Kona Waruk. Naming himself after the river Konawaruk, a tributary of the Essequibo, seems both a modest alliance of writer to place and a radical aligning of poetic voice to an environmental perspective. Looked at alongside fiction's search to 'consume its own biases' it feels like a necessary sublimation of human ego to ecosystem. The name Kona Waruk becomes an example of how to 'generate foundations of care within the vessel of place'; it establishes a further site beyond Troy, the Bering Straits and the Amazon within Harris's concern for the twinned importance of eternity and season. There is also a coda to Harris's pen-name, as the river has gone on to tell its own history of exploitation. In the late 1940s the Konawaruk river was found to have gold deposits and over a number of years was dredged to the point of being declared a 'dead' river. Only in recent years have there been attempts to restore this riverine ecosystem, as fish return to its headwaters and humans confront the costs of their biases and care for places.

The last time I spoke to Harris we talked about him leaving Guyana in 1959 for London. He remembered that he brought no poetry notebooks or manuscripts with him. While the critic and bibliographer in me regrets the absence of this material, somehow it is not wholly a loss. This is because of Harris's creative practice: his commitment to 'many resurrections of paradoxical imagination' encourages us to see traces of his poetic energies in the later work. We might ask where and when does his work break between poetry and prose? When he left Guyana? In the pages of *Palace of the Peacock*? But these questions seem irrelevant in light of his vision of fiction. The artistry that crosses both poetry and prose is the wish to 'generate foundations of care within the vessel of place', so that all will survive, thrive and be remembered throughout our many seasons.

1 Wilson Harris, 'The Writer and Society' in Tradition, the Writer and Society *(New Beacon, 1967), p. 55.*
2 Wilson Harris, 'Literacy and the Imagination – A Talk', in Selected Essays of Wilson, ed. by A. J. M. Bundy (Routledge, 1999), p. 80.
3 Eusi Kwayana, Interview with Gemma Robinson, 20 October 1998.
4 Wilson Harris, letter to Arthur [A. J.] Seymour, 26 March 1952
(A. J. Seymour Papers, University of Guyana Library).
5 Wilson Harris [as Kona Waruk], Eternity to Season (Georgetown:
the Author, 1952). Republished in Wilson Harris, Eternity to Season
(Georgetown: the Author, 1954); revised in Wilson Harris, Eternity
to Season (New Beacon, 1978).
6 Wilson Harris, Interview with Michael Gilkes, 'The Landscape of
Dreams', in Wilson Harris: The Uncompromising Imagination, *ed. by*
Hena Maes-Jelinek (Dangaroo, 1991), p. 38.
7 Wilson Harris, 'The Unfinished Genesis of the Imagination', in Selected
Essays, *ed. by A.J.M Bundy (Routledge, 1999), pp. 248–60.*
8 See Edouard Glissant on 'point d'intrication' in his Poetics of Relation,
originally published as Poétique de la Relation *(Gallimard, 1990).*
9 Stuart Hall, Familiar Stranger: A Life Between Two Islands
(Penguin, 2018), p. 61.
10 Wilson Harris, Palace of the Peacock *(Faber, 1960).*
Republished as part of The Guyana Quartet *(Faber, 1985), p. 24.*
11 Wilson Harris, note to The Guyana Quartet, *p. 9.*

Lara Pawson
On Philip Larkin

I have asked myself, Who is Philip Larkin? I have asked myself, What are his poems to me? While exploring the possibilities for answers, I have noticed that certain authors' names bring certain images to mind.

Sylvia Plath, whose name I read every time I sit at my desk because *Ariel* is one of three books upon which my laptop rests, is a length of heavy rope coiled like a python sleeping on the polished wooden herringbone floor beneath the ledge of a bay window in the back room of a large Victorian house. Derek Walcott is a cliff-top town held in the fist of the midday sun. There is blood on the track that leads to the bullring. Andreï Makine is a corridor inside an institution. All the doors are closed, and a woman and a man are walking slowly towards me, whispering to one another in a language I don't know. Lydia Davis is a white Formica table top upon which an orange biro lies beside a vase of miniature irises. Bernardine Evaristo is a line of sweating polo ponies tethered to a fence surrounding a kidney-shaped swimming pool. Teju Cole is a plate of lobster on a picnic rug. Italo Calvino, a saucer on an empty shelf.

When I try to capture the image that appears with Philip Larkin, however, another scene always gets in the way. It sweeps down, like a velvet curtain inside my brain, blocking the view to the other side.

A young woman is sitting on an old school desk, her back to the whiteboard, her knees squeezing together inside a pair of dark stretch jeans. Her feet are twitching. Sometimes, they point. The air is cold and the tip of her nose is blotchy and damp. Obsessively, she touches her face. It is alive with acne. She keeps trying to train the thick curls of her hair behind her ears and off her face, but they will spring back again and again and again. Every now and then, her eyes roll back like balls of oiled porcelain and her lashes make butterfly kisses to the air. When she speaks, her voice swells on her tongue, filling our heads with warmed honey. She is certain of her words, she is certain of her knowledge of this poet in Hull.

Until two months ago, I had forgotten I had ever studied the poetry of Philip Larkin. Then I found *High Windows* and *The Whitsun Weddings* tucked in at the far end of one of my bookshelves beside a curious pamphlet called *The Nearly Man*, which I bought for three pounds from its author, a man who told me he'd spent three years in the Royal Marines when we encountered each other beside the Thames some years ago.

I pulled these two slim collections from the shelf and, upon opening first one then the other, was confronted by my younger, curlier handwriting framing many of the poems and filling the endpapers, front and back. 'Quite a detached man.' 'NOT a love poet.' 'Gd sense of humour – great jazz fan.' 'Liked to present h.self as serious.' 'Very democratic.' 'Never too sentimental.' 'Keen on structure & order.' 'Tries to sympathise.' 'Rarely describes individuals. More often, types.' 'Grim and satirical.' 'Never married.'

Flicking through the pages, I began to remember reading these books for my English literature A-level in 1989. I was twenty-one and still unaware that I'd been fucked up by my mum and dad. (In those days, I could see how my friends' mums and dads were fucking them up, but believed my own to be the exception.) Shortly before the Easter break that year, I learned that I had been truly fucked up by my teacher when she admitted to the class she'd been teaching us the wrong texts. The wrong Shakespeare, the wrong Hardy, the wrong Chaucer, and the wrong Larkin. With less than ten weeks to go, we would start from scratch.

Our new teacher was a man. He wore leather. He blow-dried his hair.

Trying to look back, trying to recall, I see my younger, anxious self, in the suede hot pants I wore throughout much of that year, looking from this new teacher to this dead poet. My understanding of Larkin, then, was of loneliness, and of living somewhere remote, in a cold, empty flat, with hard furniture. I see him drinking tea, already cooling in a porcelain cup. I see my younger self drained of excitement and filling with dread. Larkin was always in black and white, and bald. He was quiet in a suit and tie. I didn't want to end up like that.

Turning my back on Larkin, I looked longingly to the new English teacher. This was the man who was going to rescue us, who was going to ensure we all passed our A-level English Lit. He came to work on a motorbike. He had long, wavy hair that swayed around his shoulders as he swung back and forth between the whiteboard and us. During the breaks, he talked about Aerosmith and Metallica, about Testament and Annihilator, Deep Purple and Anthrax. I have no memory of his English literature tuition at all – only a surging desire to know my heavy metal from my hard rock, my death metal from my speed and my thrash.

How strange, the passing of time.

Thirty-odd years ago, I think I thought that people who were interested in nature were a bit dull and probably rather wet. Today, however, reading 'The Trees', every one of these twelve lucid lines tilts me towards this dead male poet. Maybe Larkin was right when he described this perfectly succinct poem as 'very corny', but in our age of catastrophic climate change, his criticism looks like a luxury. Certainly, I cannot help but be moved that 'Their greenness is a kind of grief' and by 'Their yearly trick of looking new'. At least for the trees I encounter in my day-to-day life, these lines sharpen my anxiety that this year may be their last.

Because of my concern for the planet, I've not flown since the end of 2014. I do not state this to boast green credentials or to prod you with guilt – to borrow from 'Vers de Société', I don't think I'm 'Playing at goodness, like going to church' – but to share, honestly, the depths of my desperation and fear. Apart from the odd train trip to Europe, I have remained steadfast on this miserable island for the last eight years. Or perhaps it is that I have remained, miserable, on this steadfast island? I'm not sure. What I'm certain of is that I could never have imagined, in 1989, that Larkin's poems would help me confront my native land.

Apart from the printed text, page 34 of *The Whitsun Weddings* remains blank. The lack of pencil notes surrounding the verse tells me we did not have to study 'The Importance of Elsewhere'. I doubt I would have understood it back then, anyway. Aside from a couple of months working as a cleaner in the south of France, I'd not spent much time abroad. It would be another seven years before I began to live and work in places far from home, places 'To prove me separate,' places where 'Strangeness made sense.' Reading these words today, they resonate with so much strength it almost hurts. And, yes, Larkin, I agree: 'Living in England has no such excuse'. 'Here', for me, as for you, 'no elsewhere underwrites my existence.'

Yet here I am, trying to face my country head on, learning to stare, unflinching, into its parochial abyss. I never expected this journey to be a pleasing experience, but through Larkin's lens, I am at least prepared to look – and look again. *High Windows* and *The Whitsun Weddings* may have been written half a century or so ago, but the depictions of people and place – 'the sad truths of ordinariness', as Derek Walcott wrote in 1989 in the *New York Review of Books* – feel so familiar, so much part of who I am whether I like it or not, they have the effect of folding me back into this land of my birth.

Take 'Show Saturday': I have been there! As a child, out of control on my cousin's pony, careering through the boundary rope, towards the 'keen crowd'. Over the years, I have perused many 'a tent selling tweed' and stood among 'The men with hunters, dog-breeding wool-defined women, / Children all saddle-swank, mugfaced middleaged wives.' I have parked my parents at the side of the ring to chuckle at me and my dog competing for Best Behaved Hound, Best Three Pairs of Legs, and Dog & Owner Lookalike. We came third in Most Regal, a yellow rosette – and, yes, the announcements, all 'splutteringly loud'.

This England is faintly ridiculous. Larkin's gaze reminds me of the foreign correspondent, whose eyes scan a country to capture its essential characteristics for the readers back home. The locals might feel they are being mocked, but the observations are undeniable. In 'To the Sea', we can all recognise: 'The miniature gaiety of seasides. / Everything crowds under the low horizon: / Steep beach, blue water, towels, red bathing caps, / The small hushed waves' repeated fresh collapse'. Have we not all seen 'the rusting soup-tins' and, more likely today, the abandoned cans of fizzy drinks between the rocks? Amazingly, it is 'Still going on, all of it, still going on!'

It is this continuity that I find striking. The first verse of 'Here' – which triggers in my mind similar images as the opening two pages to Hilary

Mantel's novel, *Beyond Black*, mention of which always dumps me at the junction of the M25 and the M4 – captures my own journey from the north-east corner of London down to my folks in their Dorset village:

> Swerving east, from rich industrial shadows
> And traffic all night north; swerving through fields
> Too thin and thistled to be called meadows,
> And now and then a harsh-named halt, that shields
> Workmen at dawn; swerving to solitude
> Of skies and scarecrows, haystacks, hares and pheasants,
> And the widening river's slow presence,
> The piled gold clouds, the shining gull-marked mud...

I recognise in Larkin a tension – or is it a habit? – in myself. Reading 'Here', 'The Building', and 'Going, Going', I know what it is to be drawn to the urban, to these towns and cities that are stacked with 'cobble-close families' on 'close-ribbed streets', and 'raw estates' and 'high-risers', and those who choose to live on boats in 'barge-crowded water'. But, just as Larkin observed decades ago, I, too, love to 'escape in the car' to those 'mortgaged half-built edges' and beyond to the 'fields and farms'. I have noticed, the older I get, the more time I need to spend far from others, walking over open land, along cliff edges, through forests and woods. What so preoccupied Larkin half a century ago – the proliferation of 'concrete and tyres' – worries me, too, today:

> It seems, just now,
> To be happening so very fast;
> Despite all the land left free
> For the first time I feel somehow
> That it isn't going to last...
>
> ('Going, Going')

Perhaps it is no coincidence that Larkin links, in my mind, to Mantel. It is she who once said, 'When you find yourself at the centre (no longer part of the radical), start digging the ground beneath your feet.' So far as I understand him, Larkin was never, explicitly, an exponent of the radical: he always dug the native soil beneath his feet. That said, it may be, with the benefit of hindsight, that one can read the radical into poems like 'Going, Going', 'Afternoons' and 'Money', in which he makes clear his criticism of marriage and materialism, consumption and expansion, and even our obsession with growth. 'It is intensely sad.'

I confess, however, that there is a particular poem, which stands out. It is the one I most dislike. It appears to deride someone a bit like me. Reading it today, I cannot help but think of Brexit. Of course Larkin would not have known that 'Naturally the Foundation will Bear Your Expenses' could so accurately capture the Brexiters' stereotype of those of us who wanted to Remain. Nevertheless, I hold my hand up and admit that, just like the persona he attacks, I do consider most of our ceremonies to be 'mawkish nursery games'. Many a time have I expressed to my friends, 'O when will England grow up?'

So, where does this leave Larkin and me? What image does his name conjure now? I see the Union Jack beneath clouds that are barely moving in a bright blue sky. I see a field of pig sheds, full of sows grunting with piglets in mud. I see a luminescent pink sheet, beside which a young man stands. He has a thick beard and a kind face. I am looking into an old six-seater train compartment. It is empty. I am smoking. I am hoping for company. I want a walk. I want a coat. I want to sit by a fire.

GRAY BEHAGG

beautiful way to be alone

you go to the beach alone because
the sound and the light calm you down
and because it's usually a beautiful way
to be alone but today the sun is like a story
people tell about summer, people are sitting out
under umbrellas smoking blunts, drinking
coronas, everyone has a lot of people to
come with and it's the bad alone. you try
swimming but the water's full of algae
you don't usually dislike algae but today
the algae feels like it's *about you*. a couple
have come down to see the sea, no swimming
no reading no props they just came to enjoy
the beach on a day like this when the beach is
hell and you are so unaccountably
mad at them, they are dressed exactly alike,
they sit there on the stones so long you
forget about and then notice them again. you can't
imagine anything they could possibly be saying
to each other and when they leave one of them
touches her girlfriend's arm thoughtlessly just
the way she would rest her hand on her own arm
and says do you want to make the chicken or did you
buy everything for the fish

GERALDINE MONK

Chattering Charteris. Earl Sterndale, Derbyshire.

Let fly the unquiet tongue a
longing for song wells up in my throat
on such a glorious day I leave the Dragon's Back
still racked with curvature of spine.
I go straight as a die across the crossroads.

With the sun on my left and cows on
a hill so high they graze on clouds
nothing on that heady day
primed me for the drubbing pub sign
so casual in its brash ghastliness.

A headless woman in a pretty yellow
pinny carries a tray of drinks and food.
'The Quiet Woman' the pub is called
beheaded by her husband to cheers and
clinks of glass and great approval of the village.
Oh what a laugh. Let fly the unquiet tongue.

The sign emblazoned with an arch around
the absence of her head it mocks her
mute and murder: 'Soft words turneth away wrath'
'The grateful locals did a whip-round for
her headstone' says history and not for the
first time I wish history was a liar.

Let's throw slaughter to the wind and
make this a trifling thing. Everyone seems to.
My longing for song dies back into a dull
disquieting at the back of my throat.
Let fly the unquiet tongue.

DALJIT NAGRA

from *indiom*

an extract from *indiom*, a long poem featuring poets in a poetry workshop
group in Bulbul Hall who champion the merits of the eccentric, Babu
English. This scene takes place after an Intermission. Next poet around
the table recites a poem and inspires the poets with a vision.

> Next is Madam Arrgan Murrgan with her Pwdin
> Eva of a Welsh accent, plus she bulge
>> the acme of a human tum
>> that put every Hottentot butt
>> in a busted flush, is curved as
>> Blumenbach's Caucasian skulls.

> Camera Operator admiringly to Director:
> Madam Arrgan Murrgan Buddha belly is overhang
> with flesh steeped in high cholesterol, Type II syruping
> through blood pressure
> yet Madam Arrgan Murrgan is residing on green prayer-
> juice alone, solo; no apothecary, in perpetuity, requisite!
> On close inspection   she's
>> th
>> in
>> as a svelte teen,
> as that pickle temptress, Circe,
> as Anna Pavlova, that swan of dying swans,
>> who find even handstand scorpion
> a cinch. How so? Madam Arrgan Murrgan's every madam
>> as in the parable of Gita, do by doing naught
>> as by doing naught all's caught!

> Director add to Camera Operator:
> let us hear Madam Arrgan Murrgan whose bride-like score
> is soar in honeyed high-pitch high as Rabindranath Tagore.

>> Madam Arrgan Murrgan seem above seat levitating
>> like the aerial suspension of the ancient Brahmins:

you are too up hung
on the road but alter you must or how
        is it you become
spirit of branch singing bird whose yellow
        dreams are like kella
aka banana we cannot peel
yet is kohl music of pure princess di
        yes yes diana!
who is care the rickshaw driver we ride
        have asthmatic cough,
let him us deliver to chatterbox
        irani café
        so dismay
for our poets my tum is display

Madam Arrgan tum is now a magic lantern, a prototype
model, you know the sort projecting images in limelight.
So picture our madam with dark-lit face & ecstatic orbs
while her tum lead us into Mumbai, the café, the tall
ceiling, the teak, the punka, the tables thrummed with chat
& there Mr Ezekiel, in '70s, drifting his feedback Papermate
        over hemp-rag paper
        of a suck-cheek novice,
        each poet shown's Ms Anon,
        so many like her binned
        being born in this zone
        that is septically uncool
with each slide that's played
            it's always Nissim who will
        like paper aeroplanes
        give lift off; yet each poem
        become a reject wisdom
        of Hopkin, Dickinson
        at their inception,
        wet wings in the rain.

Madam Arrgan Murrgan, the way a fairground mechanic
is hush his metropolis of generator machinery to kip,
so it is, Madam Murrgan beddy-bye her magic lantern.

[...] The Madam now shows the poets a vision in chai cups like stars suspended above their heads

> In crazy cosmic present time,
> look, the shabash brilliant minds
> in own bedroom, with candle flame;
> they're young, studying to create
> a caboodle vision; they're sat
> behind teeny desk wearing cap
> & plimsolls, oh blinking hell
> it's Johann & Friedrich Schlegel;
> on another star/cuppa-skin,
> at it, Laura Riding Jackson,
> oh, & there revolving up close
> Edward Casaubon with his nose
> at the keyhole of a theorem
> pleading for his golden key home!

[...] The Madam now hovers the ultimate book above the heads of the poets, the poets are excited into a prayer

All have fall weeping on knees neath its geek force,
all fall chanting a prayer as GOLDEN BOUGH soar
> Bulbul Hall like bullion in the brill air:

you have make the world more glassy than glass,
you are bright than glass, you are colour more tropic
than glass, more telescopic than glass,
> you have annealed our mortal plot
> lo! glass where everyone's flesh
> the heart's low swinging chariot
> must find own heaven as it lift
> > past the dance of
> > sphere on sphere
> > spinning top
> > stellar bop
> > Lindy Hop!

ANDY SPRAGG

Shell grotto

These faint reflections do no harm, sound nothing,
figure anything fits in these bad times.
Left mouthing at dutiful plunder's glow,
the trappings of this stroke, all guesses left
to glisten fish scale amongst rocky pools.
Our leader, an officer, unthought of,
told when the master move was made and that.
Shout to the extent of the law, universal tidings,
conceived without windows, sound or light
when nothing comes in, bigger than you expect.
He pictured enough bodies all aflame
in the folds of the soul, I expect he was tired.
I'm sorry folks, that's all we have time for.

J.H. PRYNNE

BESIDE SEASONAL
(_maestoso moderato_)

REFLECT ONE

Rain soon in near stream, bird fresh in bush
deep winding clear shone to ours and miner
quarry flurry willow call, finding search wish
act passion relented, forgiven, as to whence
              along to sing; in tune
Pine cones bright in August, cloud arranged
glitter fringe, safe houses torrent to relayed
friendship cascade over brocaded. Willingly
intended ride outward eventual new-made
              allocate in main part
Hold up echo see eye to ear braver heat out
compensate implicit call-sign hillside waded
river flow overgrown; accept message quite
pulse meet later visited, violet maiden suits
              ramble waver cautious
Later egret bayonet, lonesome beforehand
renewal coaxial eggshells; immoderate tide
straw packing dissenting adventurous refer
toadflax flaunting uniform curlews crossbill
              singleton reprobated
Earwig meatus afflatus aloof paddock aspic
suspicious oxtail ravenous subsequent pint
birth canal or canary culinary ravel sleeved
craved mouse-tail chickweed modal fragile
              abashed music hyphen
Both twice either otherwise; documents so-
called phantom light shower low-down dice
crevice speedwell bonnie boat rowlock fate
snuff. Egregious supple auction tiffs ophitic
              shearwater, as tilting

Occulted diorite mischievous frantic penalty
canopied ultimate druse; lairs intact anklets
worthy haptic florid incessant, entire below
intervals dill trial mammoth tooth froth else
        alligator circulated bit
Prone soonest dip-stick red-brick expected
vein in bones seam aimed bramble tremble
yard-arm paving, under mission late amber
timber stack wicket lappet original cragged
        bolt inside or gatepost
Divested cost+plus entrenched, knees joist
ride the wavelet amulet spaghetti innocent
however entice waist; diction by utterance
fair to bear airways, near and far beyond pi
        circus honest clowned
Indigenous moisture. Necklace on remission
organ voluntary sentence tissue, fissure soft
promise velvet candied peel aftermath best
polymath graphite; inscript engrossed toast
        gibbous fasten iced
Crystalline entwine tar sands frenzied heads
space lattice differ, swagger water sapphire
effort lifted yellow flagpole oriole. Condoles
mournful cranesbill wellspring, dewlap alert
        concert pitch fetch
Streamline ketch fingernail kestrel followers
nervously peardrop ear-ring RNA beekeeper
steeped in grins pollen; plainchant penchant
folic indicated prize-winning brethren cream
        as eglantine, as mine.
Cyclone sealions, servile impetuous cautious
rushes green growing fawn growling python
agnate toxic surreptitious luffing & coughing
asseverated near-sighted prismatic rabbit pi
        jam-jar nightjar gated.
Or mercies adduced by remission, recipience
by patience smiling while at least unless doff

surprise beneath heathland who knew dews
moisten the eyelash one after next. Set pitch
              call oboist canoe lit
bright candelabrum unabashed, incautiously;
ride the wave thrown up in spray pyramid to
insinuate port instigate rack dock mock turtle
start out star charts look before leap year nil
              counter-sink sunk.
Fear entire deplore depth charged discounts
dash selected liqueur dispel predicament re-
freshed by arbitrage, please on both sides big
fish back in the water inventively in readiness
              as infolded by noise
For plentiful impulsions brokered by applause
both ways in grand displays, aftermath collect
to find the cause unrusted swords, untrusted
words in ever-during night: enough released,
              driving the screw, true.
When dew collects in drops as for bright sparks
in lark to market torn, in cheek outworn, so soon
the bridal of the day and night, the morning who
comes soft and blue; soever ready as for new, to
              grow to ripen fruit.

REFLECT TWO

For white mice enticed shadow self, wolfish pilfer
niece nicht zu schnell so ever true and coloured
slight, herewith eyebright fraught taught lessen
both handsome chine grimace beef; concentrate
              verified balustrade
self-taught bargain abasement lateral integument
forestry topiary dentition split first, erstwhile yet
valiant tryst attested distract abacus taken rifted
back, nick-nack off sheen persimmon moonshine
              anarchic refunded
moribund; bacchic ill-met by lunatic flight to flit,

harpoon annexed entanglement 'spooky' action
dereliction, distantiate net-zero evaporant later
mitre fossil momentum reversion, diagonal ant.
      How to know one
from next which fanciful inch trappist bee-hives,
cost lift crisped canonical dual cannon-ball well
cocktail Molotov sling call-sign tooth lost forced
ice; hand to mouth invoke henbane anciently at
      devised basilisk
dice cast-off vocalised. Rafters alabaster crucial
complicit elastic forceps thallus, all-out decretal
weaponry borrowing browning planetary gospel
redact bruised by leaf twice woven unlaced most
      fringe affright
tasted, dog's mercury fitful fever savoury tippits
'think of horses not zebras'; reindeer rained here
tearworn tea-time lion tamer trimmed, pungent
at catmint indented came and went scented in
      rhymed debate.
Imperishable feudal Urn Burial orioles golden at
velvet benefit grip tight, biblical nettle fleeter on
sipped floret scoop occident; aridity loitering plan
flaming rictus burnoose dormouse purpose for
      danger in smoke,
billow burrow or undisclosed under-foot best
current mango imago, surface cryptic furnish
impression fusion ascension peninsula glittering.
Distinct contestant vibrancy currency exchanged
      coastal boasted
adjusted childhood annoyance at mischievously
share device rejoicing, plentiful continual, go first
never worse albatross; inversion caution incidental
pylon wooded slope in shadow draw-down reflown
      nightshade,
crusade pride strontium calcifuge wage joist elbowed
aside. Each over other woken bracken turban mayo,
seldom not yet or willing indebted uplifted; mustard

orchard pilchard fulsome, chrome minnow hallowed
       in custard
shoe-horn born aloft rodent accident tape measure ore
extracted washed, dish piecrust blackbird homeward
overt soapwort, bistort; reversion attraction all when
time to fly alliance, singular appliance confidence, off
       chance tense
sibilance consistency thereon, whereto resonance pair
hybrid aromatic mimetic twin-bonding chocolate out
astute godwit flamingo fiery display radiance clouds
swallow gulp known in front; salute take parade lids
       stars wash
stubborn auburn canticles far before reed margin beds
at wind-swept ectopic lyrical hinterland, evenly trained
raffia surgical freight sutured morning at first before
hastened to pudding basin kingfisher crescent. Upon
       artery artillery
livery issuance, assiduous soft voices fishery sympathy
native furtive missive nozzle hazel dazzlement puzzle
minimal silenced aspect pandect; marooned syntactic
woodside optical canted aside suited integuments let
       runic aback
ransacked, intrigue far ahead indigenous fleece pumice
head-first lenticular ensure foaming brine at-olivenite
greedy incision wary athletic; pocket wisteria hysteric
flageolet homage press-stud cadge flavoursome figits
       argus tremendous
skippers longboat off-shore nectar innervation
tonsure femur split. Precipitate burdensome yearning
birdsong urgent chirrup, curtail invasive imminent add
mazy motion solution to plaited intendment scaped;

fast fasten clinic, beetle fertile peninsula invar steeled.

CHAD BENNETT

Queen

I have come

to set

the earth

on fire

and it

is already

burning

Abasement

Years ago – decades, if that's possible – he would join, sleepy,
every morning, my commute downtown to work, one stop
after me, headphones in, making his way with the strange,
staticky sensuality of the just-awake to the back of the crowded
bus where he would sometimes, depending on how the available
space had shaken itself out that day, drop himself beside me on the
cramped bench seat, a fog of tinny music, his leg here nearly against
mine, surely unaware of the fizzy sensation radiating like pain from
his to my thigh, to the hip, then out seemingly everywhere across a
network of nerves lighting up my body. If I would close my eyes, what
a creep I was, to the pale pink of his lips, they would be only more
present, as if gently pressing my eyelids for the duration of our four
stops together, and, creep, I would hold myself still, still as a dead
thing, which I was. We never

                              spoke. I never knew his voice. I don't
believe I once met his gaze, or he mine. I hardly knew myself then,
or knew myself all too well, who I would have to become but didn't
yet dare, each of those what must have been at least two hundred days
before I left that city and its hill. Sometimes with my eyes held shut in
the heavy air, the bus growling in descent, he would appear to me,
but with a bruised smile, torn breath, impossibly warm, or a thread
of blood from nose to throat, and through this daydream I would,
I knew, endure any humiliation for his humiliation, and, as if to
communicate this devotion to him, my leg drew incrementally toward
his, and he ignored it, if you can ignore what you don't feel, which
I know now you cannot, or can, but at what cost. Someday I will
disappear. And what I take with me who will have known, not you,
and if not you, then who. Destroy me. No. It was a short-lived
commute, little more than a year years ago. I still think of him, more
than some lovers, and should feel stupid, but don't.

GBENGA ADESINA

Dancing Othellos
after Romare Bearden

The boys, newly forlorn and unaware
move their small lakes of limbs.
In the dark, plural flowers, egg-tempera.
In the dark, a little realm of horses, eternity
of horses and the moan of water
that lingers on their lips as they run.
When the curtain rises,
the boys stretch their sinew of arms,
and paddle breathless air.
Red ovules bloom on their palms.
One boy lifts up his armpit and reveals
a lampshade: pale-pink of scar
on flesh.
Another draws his face close
to the mark of injury
as if to inhale the deeper grain of the other.
I, one among the shadows, undress and I'm not ashamed.
A kiss or a fruit passes between our mouths.
The darkness on the stage is lineage.

ALICE WHITE

Girl in the Woods

I get glimpses of her in pictures, in
a t-shirt and no underwear, before
she cared, or bareback on a horse before
the branch. Before boobs, before boys. Before
school she was everywhere, that much is sure –
before the world condensed into a shape
to fit into. Some days I can sense her:
I disappeared from a girl scout campout
to commandeer a wooden raft I found,
looking. My counsellor shook her head, just said
I wouldn't have expected this of you.
Whenever I think I've got hold of her,
she kicks my shin and wriggles from my grasp,
runs for the trees, calls back, *Try and catch me –*

JOSHUA BLACKMAN

Utopia (Draft #14)

And you can google it. A place
of preternatural bliss, the dads sound, the amenities numerous
where our caustic asides still garner applause
and wrens refuse to alight on the hateful. Scroll left
and you'll find the municipal baths, *La Séductrice*
and the mindfulness centre, with their respective
(eclectic!) architectural styles, from brutalist hulk
to postmodern. Scroll right (ignoring those
blurs by the bins) and you'll come – almost there –
to Bar Luca. In my view the best
carbonara in town. No lighting inside. All vegan.

OAKLEY FLANAGAN

[20]

My wife never said I couldn't fuck beautiful boys
when we married. Applause from the male table.
I do not say I am a they: a sore subject in this kingdom,
being his pleasure minion. The dark lady, of desire:
constituted by proximity. I scan the private members'
room like a sonnet, a woman's painted face reflected
in the table's lacquered finish, & smile, as anyone
used to working front-facing service roles is loath to.
He lectures on the correct technique to pour champagne,
restrained into glasses. I raise a toast to absent friends
in silence. He critiques: my slack wrist, pure doggerel.
Foam upsets the top. I scrape seabass up my outfit, count
sets of tailored legs gatekeeping their silken treasures.

JAY WHITTAKER

All about my other

At my other's knee / dock with the other ship / other's milk / the
other wound

otherland / others weekly / Christian others union / other superior /
how to be a good other / othering Sunday / unplanned otherhood /
bad others / negligent others / spendthrift others / stay-at-home others /
working others / absent others / holy other of God

repair the otherboard / what every other should know / others of
invention / others of necessity / Otherwell

a natural other / grand other / divine other / otherly / other courage /
other's little helper / other's ruin / others always get the blame / the
other of all wars / otherfucker

LUIS MUÑOZ, *translated by Idra Novey and Garth Greenwell*

Lodging in a Poem by Nietzsche
(O Mensch! Gib Acht!)

First he demands attention.

Of the world he later says
that it's deeper than the day.
(In the sense that it contains it?)

Later he speaks of pleasure
as deeper than pain
because it aims, above all, to persist.
(For the hopeful way it sews
what no other thread can?)

Silent

The day shod with absence,
the present arrives
like bees, wasps, flies
toward a scent.

Or perhaps there are
unsoldered links,
pincers without prey.

Elegy Often Postponed
to Maricruz Bilbao

I remember him outside of memory,
in front of me,
smiling at the sun
(white hair standing on end,
invisible water
plaiting his cheeks)
one hand shielding his eyes.

In a crowded space
(crisp voices and funnels
of people like pollen)
like the one we're walking through.
With a mixture like this,
of astonishment and street.

Agent

Since he didn't want others
to distract him,
he focused on his suffering
as if on an animal lodged
inadvertently within him.

He cared for it, attended
diligently to its every need.
The corner of his eye,
the hair of his arm, always attentive.
Any fluctuation
of his nature meant
the animal was asking for something, and he would comply,
whatever it might be.

KIMBERLY CAMPANELLO

Fault

A call was made to a team of specialist coroners who would work with
local volunteers. The team arrived and the layers were cut back. When
they reached the flesh everyone said 'I'm feeling so hungry' at the exact
same time. Later the son held her eyeball in his arms. That is the photo
I received. Afternoon passed and organs came out. It was clear this time
that the fault was not with us. Instead, the cause of death had arisen
from organisms living in the fish she had eaten. They had infiltrated
her system and destroyed her heart. The team was somewhat relieved.
She was twice as long as my house is deep. The day is remembered as
a good experience.

SAFIYA KAMARIA KINSHASA

In Bridgetown, a Man Who Hangs His Socks in a Shopping Trolley Is Saving up to Buy His Dead Mother a New Hat So She Can Finally Gain Some Control Over the Sun

in the wrong part of town night is a hunting dog
a man gave who slept in Bridgetown's stickiest circle
gave me directions out   his mother gave birth to
every version of Barbados but herself   they & we did
not exchange names   he does not believe in them
or teeth   in May he pulled them out to swallow lies
easier   he traded sweet ice for blue notes
on the weekends he fixed cars & drank beers by them
our flag has a yellow streak in the middle   no one
wants to see just an ocean

do you remember when our souls behaved like
millipedes making bridges with our bodies so we could
be in two places at once?   he asked if i could check in
on his mama   when i asked where she was it was as
though he was describing the inside of a biscuit tin
her dimples were the kind that recognised themselves
in the curves of plantain   when she sliced the necks off
the yellow ripe fruit   her dimples searched for new
mirrors   & so will this man   eventually
we just need to wait for the glass crow to stop
eating the crumbs passing through his ribs

PETER GIZZI

Dissociadelic

To be a desperate player
in the invisible world.
This is something different.
To have crossed over into ink
and to loiter and bleed out
on the occasion of the universe.
I've learned this.
My spirit broke long ago
so I won't be broken.
This is something quite different
inside the song.
Blurs. Gestures. Something loved.
Come as you are, collapsing
and thriving with endings
like beginnings.
When 8 Ball says 'ask again'.
When the day reveals
the prismatic systems of loss,
the black shimmer
on new macadam in a sun shower.
Everything always in black.
Black wax. Black dress. Black hole.
Whatever.
When you're brought to your knees,
sing a song of praise.
When you're gutted,
embrace the whorl. FTW.
There's nothing like it.

KARL KNIGHTS

My Splint Shoes

Every splint has gone through you.
How many times did I look to you
when Miss Clinton brought a chair
out for me in assemblies, bright blue
and always in the front row?
I stare at you, my querulous brothers,
on the long drives to Addenbrookes.
There you are at all my appointments,
standing guard; when the nurse takes
my weight; when the physio wants you
off, and my hammer-toes feel naked;
when the doctor asks to speak
to me alone. *You'll go up
two sizes*, the splint-maker says.
I always tried to hide your daft bulk
under long school trousers.
Every summer you had too many holes,
the splint finally speared you.
Fifteen different shops for the right fit.
I sit on the shoe-fitting bench
like a church pew. There they are
in rows, my army of familiars saying
like a dog, *Wherever he goes, I go.*

MAUREEN N. McLANE

Thursday Poem

This cool air
These cedars
This patch of ostrich ferns
in a cool morning
greening the light
toward the birds and the lakes
that hold the trees still
in their surface
A world of appearance
A ripple through
On the pavement
the frog crushed
because this is the this
and encompasses –

Could you swivel your head
like the owl who appeared
on the fence
a long snow ago
you'd be the king / queen
of circumference –
what's beyond what's behind
a matter of the existential
inner ear   a balance
the creature on one leg
calm, still, images
and the dancer there
bending a moment
toward her impossible
eternity / now. Time
to sweep away
these nouns   Time to sweep
away they say.

Open questions pound
the meat of the heart
Tender meat you sometimes eat
O heart o heart
Another living thing
    in a cage
Another dead thing held
    in the eye
the welcoming or is it abolishing eye

So Here We Are

So here we are a year later
not much to show for it
but continuing, not to resist your
prognostications for later
extinctions, the asteroid crater
a premonition of it ('We are the asteroid not
the dinosaur'). Some sixty-six million years later
what's to show for it

~ ~ ~

who gets to live
in the 21st century
who puts the shiv
in who gets to live
in collapsing civ
ilisation. Hear my quotation marks. Sorry,
all you who want to live
through the 21st century

~ ~ ~

The loon is back alone –
no mate. A grey sailboat
on the other shore. The mountain
gone in fog. The lone
kingfisher gone. Reading Thom Gunn.
O song, your historical throat.
Looking now for that loon
on the lake. Not even a boat.

~ ~ ~

but I've been wrong before
and I'm wrong now
wrong life singing from the wrong song score
wronging the after, wronging before
nevermore evermore never oh more
everyone singing from stern to bow
that I've been wrong before
and I think I'm wrong now

FORTUNATO SALAZAR

Hymn to the Dioscuri

Petite uncle actor
at anchor .and deep
Stygian acquaintance
.you and you I don't
know how you go (go
on) apart after so much
doctrine, a bed at night
a canopy in the day
.dosel .you don't dent
won't wear my print
good money, hungry
I'm about to fall into the
source of the scent .dosel
.more sighs and tears
the stairs light blue wave
pedestals más que una
estrella rayos .you don't
stint, water, tobacco, gum
.you frown, you weave.

Hymn to Artemis

The cleverness of horses is beyond description .in
the mourning of horses I feel the wickedness of the disdain
for the sand groaning of horses .the adulation of distant
unseen geese that is the inane counterpart of that disdain
.ingenia eorum inenarrabilia .cleverness of the horse Brendo
broken as a two; thrown short water; in a house of horror scores
the horse scores; I feel, O I feel for the horsey tumultuousness
the interior Brendo; the beaten by Brendo .the skill of man excelled
by that of horses; four bars; eight bars; twelve .now have reached
the chalk line; not drowning; merely stopped dead .cretam.

MERON BERHANU

Alien

Green backpack, loaded with her life.
A tiny woman standing underneath a building –
so colossal in its whiteness
it must have a heartbeat.
The gravity of the red white and
blue weighs down her footsteps, pulls
her into its orbit. Her motherland is not
a place anymore. It is something she carries –
a wound she tends to, every night.
But right now, she is here.
In this country, in this embassy –
in front of a man behind a screen and
says *I'm ready to live.* In which she means –
I want to prove that I can.

ILIASSA SEQUIN

Quintet 7

1.

overawed i' myself like you i' yourself
   oh! my seagull oh! my friend 'wings I dreamt I had'

   my own breath I wandered, the rainbows I erred
   with you replete midst shimmer midst spell I spread

asleep awake till break of death, white forgetfulness
   oh! I loved you, believe me I loved you the best

2.

Oh! pass not by ravens oh! draw not near beasts
my love is watching your deeds, break off
the raggedness, cease the gallop the greed
or this airy elfin, this starry mighty nymph
she will whip an' torture oh! yes she will

Oh! oh! for a vulture's foaming roaring kiss, the light shrinks upon my lips
I must die while still, round she haunts you thunder to thunder wind to wind

3.

who loved an' had to trust oh! to the last oh! to the last

confessions all-drear, guideless mystery paths at my wedding
he might come, wineleaves will be none only my joy's joy only
my heart, double-smitten double-slain by my own endeavour

alas, oh! oh! young brides look you here, upon the fairyland
.... so many kindled roses could not but savour ash

4.

oh! cold   oh! frozen feeling o' a sleep
to which no love no hate can reach

and oh! you so infinite, mingled in pain,
no more wait another self-rioting
self-unwanted yellow leaf dim

death oh! oh! foregoes it… off forth upon the whirlwind
it lingers it skims, it is you it is me, betrayals, vows, extinct

5.

Oh! is all forgot is all purchased by the awe

a rose a chrysanthemum, a corpse amidst the worms
a secret of counterfeiting needless eternities
an' the unknown unthought of, then oh! oh! what

if someone for want o' life, makes believe on odds
'death itself has lost'

TRIBUTES

On Roddy Lumsden and Callie Gardner

...

Fran Lock
A *Terrific Melancholy*
for Roddy Lumsden

'But poets establish what remains'
– Friedrich Hölderlin

The back blurb for Roddy Lumsden's collection, *Terrific Melancholy* (Bloodaxe, 2011), describes it as a 'book of changes, physical and emotional'. It is also a book of survivals: that which persists and that which returns; a book of traces and remains. Roddy feels to me most legibly present within the pages of *Terrific Melancholy*. This seems appropriate. When I miss him, which is often, it is to this book, his sixth, that I find myself drawn.

My own copy stores the scars of this obsessive, repetitive handling: water-warped, the laminate cracked, some pages are loose, some spotted with mildew, some stained with coffee. It is less a book now, than the tactile repository of my loss; talisman in a private ritual of remembrance. I carried it with me for months after Roddy died. I took it to Honor Oak on the day of his funeral. I sat on a bench up on One Tree Hill, reading my favourite pieces out loud. Written down this sounds half daft, the kind of self-dramatising gesture Roddy would have baulked at. I've no argument to make, except to say that in *Terrific Melancholy* there is a compelling and idiosyncratic lyric gift. Through this gift his 'best self lives on' ('A Localised History of Dry Precipitation'). On that day I wanted to honour and invoke that self against anger and sadness.

For the longest time my overwhelming feeling was one of disorientation, as I attempted to separate the collective loss of a poet and editor of stature from the loss that was mine alone: loss of my first champion, my stalwart and long-suffering mentor, my perceptive editor, my eccentric, often maddening friend. I struggled to understand just how much of this grief I was supposed or allowed to feel. Having his books – *Terrific Melancholy* in particular – helped to ease that confusion. To make it matter less. When I became overwhelmed, I'd return to this work, arrested time and again by its flair and formal daring; its distinctive mix of the meticulous and the mercurial. There's a richness to these poems, a delight and excitement in words, coupled with an acute sense of their limitations: all that language cannot do, undo, or solve.

One of the collection's most powerful and persuasive undercurrents is the imperfect ability of art or memory to capture and preserve. *Terrific Melancholy* abounds in unreliable anamnesis; in transience, amnesia, change and chance. To read the collection is to understand that any attempt to enshrine or preserve objects, people, places or relationships is doomed to failure: we can only hold them by stopping their course. We trap them in amber, they forget their functions, lose their identities. I think poetry's 'best self' is infinitely more subtle than that; not memorial at all, but relational. Roddy's poems are meant to be written about and back to, shared, taught, talked through. They animate and excite us. When we think or talk about the book, we make our way back to him.

So, let's talk: *Terrific Melancholy* is divided into three sections – four if you count the long title sequence as a discrete unit. 'From the Grave to the Cradle' opens the collection with an uneasy exploration of rebirth in many guises. I read the book before meeting Roddy for the first time in 2011. I guessed wrongly then, but I now know that the allusion belongs to the strange and stately 'Fellow Travellers' by Procol Harum: 'This life is a fable / From the grave to the cradle / Slow dance through the dark night / To the sweet light we crave.' Roddy's work is like that, buzzing with musical quotations, allusions, nods and nudges towards obscure or forgotten songs. They form part of the poetry's context and long biography. Roddy would say of his work that it was 'referential' or 'self-referential' as opposed to strictly 'confessional'; he gives little away, but these references form a kind of coterie address, a signalling back to the songs that shaped his writing and to those who shared their listening. They're an acknowledgement of influence, and they're thrilling because they show the poems' working. Perhaps more accurately they mark the moment when the poet assumes the risks of failure: that step into the dark between spectating and creating. Poets partake – with varying degrees of enthusiasm – of popular culture. Some contemporary poetry likes to elide that fact, pretends to the rarefied, bloodless, and scholarly. Not Roddy. He celebrates our status as links in a chain, as people in the world. I love the honesty of that. It's rare. Ultimately, I see these references as traces or as 'clues'; they offer a way into a Roddy poem, a light to see by or a lens to read through.

In 'From the Grave to the Cradle', by flipping that well-worn linguistic commonplace – that inescapable linear trajectory on which all of us are bound – Roddy also seems to indicate the uncanny temporalities of poetry, its ability to pivot between the temporal and the extra-temporal, to hold us, if only for a moment, outside the rational flow of time.

I have been thinking about this a lot over the last three years. *Terrific Melancholy* is dedicated to two poets – Craig Arnold and Paul Reekie – who themselves died far too young, and whose influence can be discerned throughout the text in pale ghostings, odd echoes. It isn't that Roddy writes like either of these poets, it's more that you catch a trace of them here and there: the way Arnold would suddenly zoom out from the intense scrutiny of an ordinary object or scene into a profound moment of existential disquiet, or Reekie's bruising swagger through vernacular, those cunning swerves and slant connections. Little traces, little phrasal affinities. How many of our own poems carry a similar trace of Roddy? What does this mean? Poetic influence is a game of whispers. The original voice simultaneously summoned and distorted. That's the pact: if you endure at all, you do so transmuted and scattered.

There is an anxiety – at least an ambivalence – about such literary and artistic posterity seeded throughout the collection. 'A Localised History of Dry Precipitation' makes explicit the link between the dead body and the body of work through the idea of dust. The poem begins with the words 'Posthumously published'. It goes on to describe the voluminous materials amassed by the speaker's father towards a treatise on dust; of 'the notebooks and logbooks, near two hundred / of them, dated and stacked.' Dust is 'perceptual waste' and 'residual culture'.[1] It signifies death, both the gone away and the left behind, the beginnings of neglect. Dust is a metonym for the essence of the archive, for things abandoned and long forgotten; it is also life's tactile remainder, all that persists after bodies, bloodlines, and empires have perished. From here the poem multiplies ironies in a typically Lumsdenesque fashion: the book of dust succumbing to dust. The father's 'evident plans' for his history reveal a profound failure to learn from the object of his study the futility of ambition. He attempts to catalogue and preserve a thing the very essence of which is a two-fingered salute to any such endeavour. While the author fixates on ever 'finer particularities of / dusts, their peculiarities and aberrations, lists of / their specific names in Sanskrit and the Celtic / tongues' the real world seems to slide from view. There is an estrangement between the speaker and his father, who 'circled and pet-named' each dying fly with a 'humour we had never / witnessed in our boyhoods'. Reading these lines, I see our own obsessions too. Poets are keen listeners 'for descent – all things fall – a smut, a granule'. Our attention concentrates in small things, our seeing sharpened against them. We are avid collectors of cultural ephemera; esemplastic, eclectic, a regular mischief of magpies. At our best we distil this acuity of focus into trippy nectar, but we often pursue such nectar at the expense of 'real' life.

Whatever that is. I've been thinking about this lately too. My sense of Roddy was always that he lived in and through poetry; that it was his way of belonging to the world, his umwelt. We had this in common, I think. Sometimes poetry rescues life: it provides a place where our lateral leaps of logic can be encountered on their own terms; it channels our destabilising intensities, our essential oddness, not only into 'art' but into community. But poetry can also divide us from life, become a substitute for it. As poets, our capacity to become absorbed is crucial, but our preoccupations can lead to a hopeless disconnection from other priorities, can lead us into a dark tangle of mania and isolation. To some degree we all wrestle with this, collectively and individually. Roddy resisted it with energy: he helped us along, he brought us together, he gave us social space. But it's always there: at the back of the mind. As an animating tension just beneath the surface of the work.

The above makes it sound as if *Terrific Melancholy* were a morose and brooding book. It's not. It's too inventive for that. In 'From the

Grave to the Cradle' persistence and change are evoked in dust, in the pre-born hovering at the edge of limbo bracing themselves for the shock of re-entry; as a crime scene's evidentiary gleanings, the micro-organisms teeming in yeast, in lapses of memory, heavenly eternities, in fleeting moments, in triumphant returns to the world. My favourite of these has always been 'The World', probably because I know keenly that desire to scrub out and start again. And who wouldn't want their 'enemy distilled to a tot / and swallowed / the sauce will be smoky / the ale fierce and cold'? There's a longing in this poem so intense that it seems to transcend wishful thinking, becoming instead the occultist's act of pure will. It seems entirely feasible that the speaker will return, rising from 'the sweet bath' of turning surf with 'hands high'. I'm not sure what creates that effect. The imperative tone of the opening line: 'when I return'? And maybe the structural looseness of the poem, its lack of capitalisation or punctuation, the lines drifting apart across the blank space of the page. There is something spectral about it: the words seem to be in the process of drawing together, they have not yet coalesced into a definite shape. There's hope in this lack of fixity. Nothing is settled, everything possible, the old rules are suspended. Yet in the eleventh line we come to the stark declaration: 'and I will not fear women / laughter / human touch', and the poem pivots; we suddenly understand this impossibly utopian future as a way of expressing a difficult, lonely present, where wiping away and starting from scratch are the only available forms of escape.

Although the book is replete with such moments, and Roddy's poetic subjects are often caught in the same unenviable impasse, the protean nature of his language, and the poems' shape-shifting engagement with form prevent the work from feeling bleak or stale. It isn't only that Roddy makes archaic or unusual choices – 'thrip', 'glisk', 'foisoned', 'cutled', 'ochlophobic', 'catachresis' – but that the use of words from across different lexical fields – some decidedly 'unpoetic' – create glitches, moments of arrested and retuned attention. Roddy understood intimately, better than anyone I have ever known, the process by which language is reinvigorated, how it feeds from and sustains itself. A number of poets are in love with the strange or difficult word for its own sake. All good, but can you see those same poets reaching for 'Fetherlite', 'Tizer', 'Maxwell House' or 'Meccano' should their poem call for it? Roddy had his biases – many will remember the infamous Banned List – but he wasn't one to reject any word out of hand; he seemed always to know by some highly developed sixth sense what his poems needed, be that a dialect word, an anachronism, a well-known brand name. If *Terrific Melancholy* is a book of changes, these changes take place within language too. Language preserves the past and mutates it; makes the past present in the present, collides or layers both place and time. I have always admired Roddy's enthusiastic willingness to revel in the plasticity and suppleness of language. He does this too with form: inventing, combining and reshaping the poem on the page. Roddy's imagination is so restless and alive that it can never be contained within one style, within one single solid structure.

'From the Grave to the Cradle' ends with 'Bowdler in Heaven', connecting again the idea of posterity, eternity and state-change to language and the scene of writing. Thomas Bowdler is best known for his expurgated edition of Shakespeare, that is Shakespeare with the sex and violence omitted. Accordingly, his heaven is 'iceberg sweet, unalloyed, harm on hold.' The piquant twist is typically Roddy: trapped in an odour-neutral paradise of his own making, Bowdler is driven to distraction with boredom. He longs for 'an eye gouged out / or a spill-breasted milkmaid touching her toes'. The poem wants life and literature with all the 'dirty thrill' kept in. It's a warning of sorts, I think, that stinted language produces stunted imaginations, sad abbreviated souls. And vice versa.

The second section, 'Hair and Beauty' is often described as a miscellany, which in the strictest sense I suppose is true, but the term always sounds a little disparaging to me. This section certainly demonstrates Roddy's flair and versatility as a poet, but I don't want to reduce him to a litany of cheap tricks, like a magician producing coloured scarves from his sleeve. I've been trying to remember how it struck me the first time I read it. I recall my surprise – although why I should have been surprised, I don't know – at finding the Hiberno-English 'fluthered' in 'The Crown'; the way 'The Crown' is followed by 'El Sombrero de los Reyes', the only poem in the collection that rhymes, and which proceeds by self-contained tercets; the way this poem suggests itself as a song sung by that same 'fluthered king' wending his way home through Blackheath. It has a drunken, oddly kilter'd metre;

it seems to suggest a teasing and not necessarily benevolent intimacy. The poem links seduction and deception in subtle, slightly disturbing ways: 'scam of fire', 'smudge of alibis', 'a secret spoken is a lie'. Roddy also evokes 'rumour' and 'clue,' completing not only the lover's toolkit, but the poet's. The ambiguous addressee is 'tightly' lined with 'saline, silt and serpentine', all stinging salt and snakiness.

Misaligned, hopeless or doomed desire snakes through this section, building to a crescendo in the title sequence, which leads the reader through an actor's long infatuation with his younger colleague. It's an astonishing poem, a sustained and often painful meditation on unrequited love and the slow decline of creative and sexual power. It is foreshadowed by earlier poems: 'Duology' where the speaker turns from his contemplation of Dalí's *Le jeu lugubre* to reflect that 'we age: easier to love, harder to desire', or '1979', which swerves from a carefully visualised description of a clandestine tryst to the couple quietly talking of 'how people form a cue to exact or escape love', their conversation dying out into haunting dread. Then there are the squeamish insectile similes, where attraction is figured as feeling like 'a wasp on sellotape' ('I Will Not Marry You') or the way 'you'd slip a hand into a gloveful of cockroaches' ('The Shuffle'). 'Grit lurks in the honey' the speaker reminds us in 'People, Their Wretchedness' a poem in which even meetings with strangers end in 'retributory showdowns'.

Against the exploration of abject desire, Roddy plays out a preoccupation with our fallible mythologising, whether of ourselves, our relationships, our heroes. While the poems in this section feel more vulnerable and exposed than in his other books, Roddy undercuts his own confessional tone by proving such an unreliable biographer to 'Olivier', 'Kerouac', and the song thrush ('Ten Things You Ought to Know About the Song Thrush'). He's well aware of the poet's propensity to transform everyday pain into sweeping narrative; to exaggerate, to dramatise, to embroider. *Terrific Melancholy* enacts this process but is also a mode and a commentary on it. This allows Roddy, as he often did, to walk that tightrope between disclosure and restraint. I often wondered – but I never worked myself up to ask – whether that's why he chose an actor for his speaker in 'Terrific Melancholy'? Acting is a profession that straddles artifice and truth; that obliges its practitioners to live through and to live on through their masks, their scenes. The poem is relayed in scenes, in short and highly vivid self-contained tableaux. As I read this piece for the first time, I remember thinking that an actor is already insubstantial, a ghost or a shell, reading someone else's lines, negotiating emotion with gestures borrowed and rehearsed. My sharpest, most critical feeling was that poets are like that too. I have asked myself a number of times how much of this speaker is Roddy: Roddy playing the part of an actor playing a part. Then I read the fifth scene, which references the glorious 'Blue Black Grape' by Shelleyan Orphan and that closes with the lines: 'wondering is it the sea that sieves / the stones or the stones that sieve the sea' and I think maybe fifty-fifty. And I think it doesn't matter either way.

The final section is 'Steady Grinding Blues', a reference to an astonishing blues number I know best as performed by Dorothy Baker. When I first read *Terrific Melancholy* I didn't appreciate this section, or its interaction with that most pervasive culture myth: the American road trip. Once I grasped that fact, the poems made more sense to me. I track Roddy's halting transit across the United States once more. He seems to live intently, immersed in his surroundings, but it doesn't sound like fun. There's an odd quality to the poems of lag or separation. I used to think that maybe the American real was being mentally measured against its legend and found lacking, but reading the penultimate poem 'Water Street Drop-off' again, I wonder: is it the speaker who is being measured up, who is measuring himself, against the legacy of James Merrill? Against America itself, which demands a bigness, a resilience of which he is incapable? There's an uncanny feeling, of inhabiting the same space, constrained by or condemned to enact the same gestures. It's a possession the speaker is unequal to.

Which is where I came in: survivals, persistence, inheritance, myth. And Roddy collides the idea of literary immortality with the physical fact of the perishable or ailing body, so that an 'exact pain' is caught 'tombstoning from temple / to jaw'. The intransitive verb somehow adds to that sense of doubling, blurring, dislocation. Tombstone summons an image of literal grave-markers, but 'tombstoning' is the practice of jumping into the sea or a quarry from a cliff or tor; the jumper enters the water vertically straight, like a tombstone. The verb ascribes the pain an agency, even a dynamism or recklessness, the speaker himself does not possess. I also found myself thinking irresistibly of Tombstone, Arizona, an infamous frontier town now a tourist hotspot with staged gun battles and a replica gallows. America seems to exist in that space throughout these poems, suspended somewhere between the museum and the theme park, haunted by the ghosts of itself.

Perhaps I still haven't got to grips with those poems. I don't mind that. I take them slowly; I allow myself to make fresh discoveries on each return. Roddy is a poet who makes that possible. Each encounter is so much more than repetition, so much more than dully comforting. To read Roddy is to feel provoked, tantalised, beguiled, frustrated, seduced and outsmarted. It's to want to know. That was very much Roddy as a person too, I think. He inspired affection, curiosity, he inspired us to write. He also inspired us to read, to listen, to watch, to observe, to participate in life and in each other. He reminded us always that we 'are not hopeless who do not know hope' ('The Sign of O'). More accurately, that hopelessness isn't the end, that life matters, however straightened or imperfect or short.

I don't fancy some trite comment here about how he 'lives on' ('A Localised History of Dry Precipitation') through the work of others. It's true, up to a point, but if there's any justice in the world, Roddy Lumsden will outlast us all, and those who have need of it will be discussing his vital, necessary poems long after we have gone.

1 *C. Nadia Seremetakis,* The Senses Still: Perception And Memory As Material Culture In Modernity *(Taylor & Francis, 2019).*

CAConrad
Callie Gardner, I Want to Keep Speaking with You
for Gloria Dawson

Poet Callie Gardner's sudden death on 8 July 2021, is still difficult to believe. What follows is a conversation with Callie's extraordinary collection, *Naturally It Is Not: A Poem in Four Letters* (the 87 press, 2018). They were among the finest poets I have had the privilege to know and read.

> if there would no longer
> be anything but differences, in that final term
> of fragmentation, where does persistence of desire go?
> ('springletter', page 8)

Dear Callie, is desire still within each fragment, and is it that very desire where the strength lies to call the shards back home? Could desire itself end its given forecast of scarcity? We say Isis put Osiris back together, but She had much help from Nephthys, Thoth, and Anubis, working their delicate magic to stitch the beloved's body back to wholeness.

> with wind blowing in the same bare place
> they can find a spirit within themselves
> of the eye and location
> ('summerletter', page 69)

In an essay about breaking your grandfather's reading lamp handed down to you from your grandmother, you wrote, 'When we attribute a particular relation to objects, they embody the success or failure of that relationship.' Regardless of the blowing wind, how still would we need to stand to become a location? What success would the spirit have in not abandoning us but insisting on filling us, being part of us until the location that is us disappears?

we were larval once
but without exchanging a cell
somewhere in this circumnavigation we became
in the creaking ancient timbers of shipped steel
just worms

('summerletter', page 61)

(I light a candle, read this stanza aloud three times, 'we were larval once...') Thank you, Dear Poet.

what would it mean to have 'wept'?
i understand crying intellectually
but to be at home with one's own brackish waters
i think would be to have one's own complex of self
be like the lochs that
unmappably, unprovably, unundertandably
dot the alien landscape here

('summerletter', page 72)

Near the Temple of Mithras, in the middle of London, is a sculpture by Cristina Iglesias called *Forgotten Streams*. It is bronze cast to look like the twisted roots and silt of the River Walbrook that flowed during the Roman occupation of Britain. Buried for centuries beneath the city's construction, an artist gave us back the flow once hidden.

under the influence of wild ink
the waterfall seems to reverse itself
when i wake up and inhabit language
i bear a wise thing and abut it with my hol'd body

('summerletter', page 59)

Dear Callie, you are the wild ink! How do I put this? I have been coaxing language to inhabit me; yes, that is what I mean. In California's Mojave Desert, I fed the wild animals around my cabin each day and night. When the coyotes arrived, I began writing while scratching the back of my ears. I rubbed just below my navel with the lizards; the

kangaroo rat got my left nipple, pushing the wild world onto me for
the poems.

> where the transhistorical sex glut
> has something to say i will listen; otherwise
> the power of sating, reserved for queer protoplasm,
> relies on its regulation, a suite of rules
> that are coming out to parse significant waves.

('springletter', page 16)

Dear Callie, the last time we spoke, you smiled and nodded when I
said Heterosexual Violence should replace the word 'homophobia', and
we should always capitalise it. It is April 2022 when I write this, and
the UK government has partially outlawed 'conversion therapy', still
allowing this Heterosexual Violence against trans children to continue.
The entire LGBTQ community needs to rise up! I think of all the gays
and lesbians I have argued with over the years who said, 'When we
have gained more rights for our community, we can turn our attention
to trans rights,' to which I always angrily replied, 'We trans and queer
people ARE part of OUR community!' We need to stand together.

In the United States this month, there are new anti-LGBTQ laws
criminalising queer bodies and lives, deeming us subhuman in Florida,
Idaho, Ohio, Oklahoma, and Texas. We will not be lonely in the face of
their fascist tyranny! We must not splinter under their violent fist! We
will allow no one to erase the T and Q from LGBTQ! We must treat any
lesbian, gay, or bisexual person attempting to erase us during these
brutal right-wing campaigns with the exact vengeance we give to the
mob of sinister Christian lawmakers plotting against us! And yes, there
are plenty of thoughtful and kind Christians who do not support this
cruelty. Still, I remember when we spoke of the brand of Christianity in
America as 'witch-burning Christians', you said that their population
was also growing in the UK.

A heterosexual friend said to me recently when I was sharing my
anger about these new laws, 'Everyone has problems, you know, not
just queers!' I calmly and slowly said, 'I need to not speak to you for
several months to know if I will ever speak to you again.' I have dreamt
of my hair catching fire, and I let it burn with no attempt to put it out.

love's only love when alteration finds,
   unbends with the all-retentive improver
          that's found in sacked temples,
astrological with the cut moon in gemini.

('winterletter', page 124)

Dear Callie, you read your breathtaking poem, 'LOVE & RAGE, & RAGE,' when we performed in Manchester with the brilliant poets Sascha Aurora Akhtar and Sara Crewe. The four of us entangling our vibrations will always be one of my favorite memories of poetry. It was two months before reports of the first Covid-19 cases.

who's this little womb?
abscess a passage, declare a vair
squirrel weakening,
      arc healthy
i care what you link around
      me

('winterletter', page 137)

Dear Callie, my boyfriend Tre and I read this book aloud after you died. Queer lovers reading your words together compounds the knowing. We were in the Rocky Mountains of Colorado in search of the much-fabled mountain peak whose twilight's optical illusion makes the stars appear to be drawn down and surround you. We had just finished cooking our dinner on an open fire, smoke filling our hair. When I told him that I was writing this today, he asked if I would mention his favorite stanza that begins, 'who's this little womb?' Let me bring him into this conversation, shoulders that have pushed me uphill more than once, fastening our love.

impeach blossoms:
      they have served their notion well,
      but now fall bitterly, soil
      the pants of spring.
      the hairy art of leaving

('winterletter', page 140)

Dear Callie, I have no interest in developing a healthy relationship with death. I reserve my health for the living, so I will not stop speaking with you whenever I read your poetry and essays. I am grateful for this opportunity to write to you today. I hope it encourages readers to seek out your extraordinary book published by the 87 press. May reincarnation be true, and may we both be poets and friends again in the next life that we meet. Until then, missing you will continue to miss you.

LEAPING, FIERCE ARROWS

Vivek Narayanan, After, *New York Review Books, £20.00,*
ISBN 9781681376462

Tishani Doshi writes about a fresh reanimation of the *Ramayana*

. . .

It may seem questionable to write a five-hundred-plus-page book of poems in conversation with Valmiki's *Ramayana* given that countless interpretations of the poem already exist, but especially because its eponymous hero, Lord Rama, has become the poster boy for India's right-wing BJP government – the rallying cry of 'Jai Shri Ram' (Hail, Lord Ram) being chanted by saffron-flag waving Hindutva mobs who are bulldozing Muslim homes and desecrating mosques across the country as I write. The poems in Vivek Narayanan's *After*, however, are masterfully aware in terms of tone and the 'time-spirit' ('Some Omens') – leaning into the wonderful slipperiness of epic time, while being fully cognisant of these current fractious times. In a preface, Narayanan writes that his goal was to 'reanimate' Valmiki, not by carrying over or translating in a traditional sense, but to engage in a more open way. The result is a collection of leaping, fierce poems that move in several directions, leaving the reader besieged and dazzled in equal measure.

As Sanskrit's adikavya or first poem, it's perhaps inevitable that the Ramayana would have this amazing capacity to regenerate itself like a sea sponge. A.K. Ramanujan famously said that no one in India or Southeast Asia ever reads it (or the *Mahabharata*) for the first time. The stories are simply there, 'always ready'. Even if you've never read a version from cover to cover, *Ramayana* transmission operates through a kind of osmosis, the characters are familiar to you, and there's a chance you may know more about them than they do themselves. Rama, for instance, the OG ideal man-king, curiously lacks access to his own interiority, and must listen to his own story from his estranged sons in order to experience epiphany. Scholars of the *Ramayana* have commented on Valmiki's non-linear, digressive, frame-within-frame writing approach, so there's a lot of this hall of mirrors déjà vu feel, partly because themes of exile and return are so strong in the *Ramayana*, and partly because the poem exists across such a multiplicity of forms – dance, theatre, painting, comic book, television serial – so the characters are alive in the house of mirrors with you, making the same mistakes again and again, forging a sense of timelessness into the bones of the poem.

Narayanan matches this dizzying story-without-closure effect with the sheer scale of his project, using no full stops, just blank spaces, which I interpreted as indicators to jump, pause, breathe. There are broad swathes of landscape, rasa, time zone that the poet navigates us through but there's also attention to miniature and the lyric. Here is the poet on the outskirts of Delhi, noticing how 'the startle of dusk continued to creep' ('A Ramayana on the Delhi Ridge (2)'). And here is the poet wrestling with that upper caste language he's been running from his whole life: 'If I were writing in Sanskrit / I'd open with landscapes / of ravishable beauty' ('The Arrow'). Much in the way that Velásquez challenged the idea of who is watching whom by painting himself into *Las Meninas*, and the way Valmiki is immortalised by bookending himself into key events of the *Ramayana*, Narayanan too ghosts along the margins of his poems as a minor character – backpacker sceptic engaged in philosophical diagnosis of a country going to shit – shifting and widening the scope of what we consider inside and outside as he travels along.

For me the most powerful part of *After* was the third section, 'War', which is surprising, given I skipped over most of the battle scenes in

War and Peace in order to get back to the ballroom. Tolstoy didn't have a simian army though, which to me is the most radical and imaginative element of the *Ramayana*. The simians who do battle in *After* are breathtaking, more noble than any of the gods or humans. In 'Know Your Enemy (KYE)' we have 'limb-stripped lion-like' Nala, 'red yellow filament of lotus tail' Angada, Chanda, Kumuda, and on and on, until we arrive at the great general Hanuman, who can shrink himself into the smallest hole or grow to the size of a mountain at will. This monkey battalion is the backbone of an epic which considers violence the source of its ars poetica. The story goes that Valmiki was watching two sarus cranes in the act of lovemaking when a hunter's arrow suddenly pierced the male, leaving the female devastated. Valmiki cursed the hunter for causing such sorrow (shoka), and the curse came out in the form of a metre (shloka), which he then used to write the whole *Ramayana*. Narayanan employs his own hypnotic beat which thuds through the book, not circular so much as jagged and open-ended, gathering force, escalating, dropping, gathering.

Reality and myth collide frequently in this collection, perhaps nowhere more explosively than in 'Poem Without Beginning or End', where Narayanan integrates Valmiki's scenes of war with reports of killings and torture performed by the Indian state in Kashmir and against Maoist insurgents in the central forests of India (also the site for the forest action in the *Ramayana*). By bringing the pared down language of obituaries and disappearances from his sources ('Comrade P. had studied BEd and hailed / from a poor family of Vargal village') to the language of poetry ('hillocks are lovely things for firing ranges'), and by hammering out this strange and terrifying dissonance for 150 pages, Narayanan collapses boundaries, connects sacred geography to real geography, and traps us in a net of horrors that refuses to relent.

If we were living in different times, I may have dwelt upon Narayanan's dexterity for play, his penchant for tenderness – a poem about his father's heart surgery quite undid me. But we are in a moment when Mughal history and the poems of Faiz Ahmed Faiz are being eradicated from Indian syllabi, where a 725-foot statue of Lord Ram will be erected in his fabled kingdom, Ayodhya, already the site of longstanding Hindu-Muslim conflict. Mythmaking in India is no longer about converting sorrow to poetry but about bulldozing dissent and solidifying a reductionist idea of Hinduism in order to set up a Hindu state or Ram Rajya.

The thing about endurance though, is that it is most enduring when it makes room for doubt. The *Ramayana* flourishes precisely because it allows for questions. In some tellings, the villain is the hero, in some, the chaste wife is not so chaste. Over centuries there have been a circle of doubters, devoted gadflies like Vivek Narayanan, who have intervened and prodded, renewed and enlarged the poem to include the concerns of their time and ensure this great work remains alive and unfinished. 'They trip us up / the ancestors   Don't mean to but // they do' ('The Bridge'), Narayanan writes, echoing Larkin, one of the many poets who enliven the pages of this ambitious collection, boomeranging us into a shaky future with the hope that 'we'll draw a trace of us / to find our way back.'

Tishani Doshi's most recent collection A God at the Door *(Bloodaxe, 2021) was shortlisted for the 2021 Forward Prize for Best Collection.*

MIDNIGHT IN PARIS

Hope Mirrlees, Paris: A Poem, *Faber, £9.99, ISBN 9780571359936*
Gloria Gervitz, Migrations: Poem, 1976–2020,
translated by Mark Schafer, New York Review Books, £9.99,
ISBN 9781681375700

Tapasya Narang on modernism and foremothers

. . .

Even though it arguably paved the way for modernist works such as T.S. Eliot's *The Waste Land* and more, Hope Mirrlees' remarkable book-length work *Paris: A Poem* has hitherto circulated in limited runs and has remained inaccessible to a wider readership. This latest edition has been produced to mark the centenary of the first publication of Mirrlees' important poem by Virginia and Leonard Woolf's Hogarth Press in 1920.

In their introduction to *A History of Irish Women's Poetry*, Ailbhe Darcy and David Wheatley canvas an argument that posits how, unlike male writers who may wish to overcome the anxiety of influence of their forefathers, women authors look to foremothers who have successfully occupied the male-dominated space of publication and 'legitimise the business of writing' – for women writers, the question of literary lineage is more fraught given limitations placed on them through gender constructs and social expectations. Mirrlees did not occupy the public sphere at the outset and her work was first produced by Woolf, who, as reported by Deborah Levy, hand-sewed 175 copies of *Paris* in her home, in 1920. Woolf's presumed commitment to the preservation of a female author's writerly genius for women successors is revisited here in the making of the current edition. It reproduces the cover of the original productions by Hogarth Press that fashioned geometrical water brush strokes, meant to connote the abstract and modernist quality of the poem. The edition includes Levy's foreword that celebrates the experimental and polyphonic aspects of Mirrlees' poem. It also contains Julia Briggs's annotations to the poem that appeared in her 2007 anthology, *Gender in Modernism*, and Sandeep Parmar's commentary on her life and works in the afterword (Parmar edited Mirrlees' *Collected Poems*, 2011).

The new edition helps to underline Mirrlees' still relevant challenge to conventional aesthetics as well as her skills in rendering a perceptive portrait of a modern city. The opening of the poem, 'I want a holophrase', sets the tone as she presents Paris in the wake of World War I. Speaking of Parisian theatre, Mirrlees states: 'The unities are smashed, / The stage is thick with corpses'. Similar aesthetic rupture informs her work. She uses fragmented sentences, typographical effects, roaming line breaks, colloquialisms, found conversations, and unusual metaphors to draw attention to the effects of war on individual lives. For instance, while representing children who would have been recruited to become soldiers, she enacts the dizziness that their sight evokes: 'Little boys [...] ride round and round on wooden horses until their heads turn.' The carousel image throws light on Mirrlees' impressionistic style: she does not provide a constitutive representation but captures fleeting realities. The poet also subverts the grandiose to mark a fragile moment in history: 'The Louvre is melting into mist.' Her vision further focuses on the convergence of several cultural influences in Paris, owing to its imperialist history, and an emergent commodity culture:

It is pleasant to sit on the Grand Boulevards –
　　　They smell of
　　　Clocae
　　　Hot indiarubber
　　　Poudre de riz
　　　Algerian tobacco

There is active questioning of language's ability to describe traumatic historical events, a questioning that was to become vital to the modernist movement. (Mirrlees' use of brief notes anticipated Eliot's.)

The late Mexican poet Gloria Gervitz's long poem, owing to its prioritisation of women's perspectives and its experimental stance, reads like a response to Mirrlees' poem. *Migrations* sprawls over 260 pages and presents poignant glimpses of female sexuality, desires, narcissism and relationships with the maternal other without glorifying or idealising womanhood. Mark Schafer's translation retains linguistic and visual experimentation, and the connotative quality of Gervitz's language: 'in the migration of red carnations where songs burst from long-beaked birds / and apples rot before the disaster'. We are in the realm of imaginative retreat into an intriguing landscape.

Further in the poem, 'migration' begins to refer to adoption of influences from literary predecessors, movement of words and phrases within the poem and Gervitz's Jewish ancestors' emigration from Eastern Europe to South America as well as her own eventual migration to New York from Mexico. The palimpsestic quality is characteristic of this poet's work as she connects sexuality, loss and mourning with the larger philosophical quests of seeking meaning in existence: 'she thrust her existence inside me / darkest roses sprouting in memory'.

Despite her allusions to traditional or canonical forms, such as Kaddish and Zohar, Gervitz rewrites rituals to describe deeply felt personal experience. For instance, she finds equivalents to the processes of rebirth, sexual union, and revelation in masturbation. ('It's like a dialogue between two who are in fact one.') Epiphanic moments – 'the voluptuousness of being born again and again / static ecstasy' – emerge out of her solitary acts and the 'fermentation of silence': 'I spread my legs beneath the bathtub faucet / gushing water falls / the water enters me / the words of the Zohar spread open.'

The author's representation of her paternal grandmother, her mother and herself signify a complex resilience as well as vulnerability, forged in the face of orthodoxy. By continually repeating her grandmother's words in the poem – 'dream that the dream of life is beautiful my child' – she engenders a sense of a constant struggle for the renewal of hope. Gervitz also addresses her mother's death quite blatantly and presents the extent of her tragedy: 'and the body withering / and smelling of urine // and the girl who cried as she clasped her dead mother / is still crying inside me.' She strikes a cautious balance between representation of the gravity of tragic realities and her resistance to devastating forces, asking 'am I the one opening / to this body of mine'?

In a sense Gervitz, who died this year at the age of 79, has applied the spirit evident in Mirrlees' text and furthered the inquiry to things that may not have been permissible a century ago. Both have produced seminal texts addressing the limitations of conventional forms and, therefore, conventional roles. The current editions perform the crucial task of introducing these texts to a wider readership and providing access to extremely persuasive modes of experimentation and social critique, extending the sense of a female modernist literary lineage beyond present uncertainties.

Tapasya Narang lectures at the School of English, Dublin City University.

A LITTLE RIP IN THE SURFACE

*Queering the Green: Post-2000 Queer Irish Poetry, ed.
Paul Maddern, Lifeboat Press, £15.00* ISBN *9781916222830*

Ben Townley-Canning on a landmark anthology

. . .

In his introduction to this vital anthology, poet and editor Paul
Maddern declares: 'This anthology is a celebration of queer creativity.
Let's revel in the moment'. And what a 'moment' these first two decades
of this century have already been for queer people in Ireland.

In his introduction, Maddern talks about the pivotal shifts in Irish
society that culminated in the vote for same-sex marriage in 2015, a
referendum that saw the moving spectacle of the young Irish diaspora
returning home. By coming back, many travelling for thousands of
miles, these people were voting for LGBTQ+ equality, of course, but
also for a young, modern, global Ireland that represented them, headed
up by the first out Taoiseach, Leo Varadkar, a celebratory moment, he
argues, regardless of politics. At the same time, Maddern also makes
the case that nothing is perfect and it would be foolish to ascribe some
queer utopia to a place where life for queer people can be – and in many
places still is – blighted by violence and discrimination. At the time of
writing, communities of Ireland have been shocked by a series of violent

homophobic murders and attacks in Sligo and Dublin. Internationally, there has been a pushback, through various legislative reforms in countries such as the US, against LGBTQ+ rights. Even in the UK, the government's attempt to tackle conversion therapy has been marred by appalling transphobia. We are in need of hope, therefore, both at home and abroad and these thirty-one poets offer some consolation and joy to both queer and straight readers alike.

As with all anthologies, perhaps this book works best when dipped in and out of, since four hundred pages covering the vast array of queer experiences can feel unwieldy at first. But one could argue that the essence of the anthology is best represented by the two poems from two of Ireland's most exciting young poets, Padraig Regan and Rosamund Taylor, which bookend the selection. Regan, whose debut collection *Some Integrity* (2022) featured their powerful and often startling poems on the body and death, opens the anthology with 'Salt Island', a poem that depicts the poet as kilted and celebratory, gleefully strutting across the coastal hills of Ireland with an unabashed self-confidence in themselves but also a strong sense of belonging to the landscape they inhabit, a landscape which they are primed to harness:

> I walked over
> the hill with my kilt flapping
> & thought
> *wow! all this for me?*

In 'Salt Island', the speaker longs to re-appropriate the traditional; they want to 'make a gothic of it all' by celebrating the gloomy weather, the 'weird kinks and angles' of the coastline, and 'arthritic fingers' of the trees. But they are only to be thwarted by the returning sun (and their subsequent desire for ice-cream). Days later, while poring over photos, the voice of the poem returns to this celebration of queerness:

> I see that my red tartan
> clashed with the grass so perfectly
> I wonder if I intended to be the punctum,
> the little rip in the surface
> where my eye might snag.

There's a clear-eyed enjoyment of queerness here: a lack of shame and a rejection of imposed assimilation that is thrilling. Regan canonises their 'little rip' across mainstream society's rules and regulations with such a joyful sense of mischief that the reader, regardless of their own confidence (or indeed sexuality) will be taken along for the ride. I most certainly was. These moments are echoed throughout the book, with celebration countering the traditional handwringing about sexuality we've been taught to expect and the poems singing off the page.

As if to sum up how the LGBTQ+ community are not one homogenous mass, the anthology's closing poem, 'Pride 2017' by Rosamund Taylor, is at first glance less concerned with assimilation and forges its own path. Taylor's poem is as political and radical as Regan's, managing to recognise past activists whose work paved the way for her marriage becoming legal, whilst looking to the future with hope (and recognising her own part in moving queer history forward):

This is old as kissing –
two bodies of the same kind

loving one another. We are new
because promises we made bind us
in law as well as love.

By having these two poems punctuate the anthology, Maddern is pitching modern queer poets as able to not only recognise and celebrate their own communities, but also pay respect to those gone before and continue the struggle for equality. By beginning the anthology at the year 2000, Maddern and many of the earlier poets pay their respects to those responsible for changes made in Irish society, both in queer politics (homosexuality was only decriminalised in 1993) and the wider politics of the region (the Good Friday Agreement was signed in 1998). The year 2000 seems to be a good line to draw in the sand; a cultural reset for queer rights in a now forward-looking country.

Ireland is, of course, famed for its nature poets – from W.B. Yeats and Seamus Heaney to more recent work by writers such as Jess McKinney – and it would be unthinkable for a modern Irish anthology not to feature at least some writing about nature. Reflecting the blossoming (pun intended) of queer nature poetry, there's a broad selection of work that breathes new life into familiar territory. Michael McKimm's 'Daffodils' is the perfect embodiment of this, picturing the ubiquitous flower as a 'singular announcement' of spring in a celebration that is a fresh take on the Wordsworth classic. McKimm expertly balances the queering of language itself (blooming bulbs become 'mines'), whilst also subverting traditional subject matter, before bringing in a meditation on queer experience that feels personal as a kind of crowning tier.

It's hard not to find the closing of this poem especially moving in the breathless, run-on nature of lines largely shorn of punctuation in which flowers dart for the sky from the darkness:

snow-survivors reaching heads up to the trees
with a raucous here we are we made it please make room
we are the sunshine fallen from the sky, we are
the darkness let to bloom.

For Seán Hewitt, whose *Tongues of Fire* (2020) made him one of Ireland's most exciting contemporary poets to write about nature, the queering is even more explicit. In Hewitt's poems nature is reclaimed, as it is in Regan's 'Salt Island', from a predominantly heteronormative gaze. In 'Dryad', the speaker visits a wood that he himself helped to plant as a schoolchild and recounts his life experiences: 'Every time I go back, I see a part / of my life laid out, still growing in a field.' One such recollection is an experience of having sex under the forest canopy since it was the only space available to him:

Here was so unlike the places other people went,
a place without doors or walls or rooms.
The black heavy-leafed branches pulled back

like a curtain and inside a dark chamber
of the wood, guarded, and made safe.
The bed was the bed of all the plants

and trees, and we could share it.

By equating himself with the trees and plants, the speaker is equating queerness with nature, mounting a direct repudiation of the often-parroted homophobic assault of 'it's not natural'. Such gestures further suggest to readers new ways of reading older Irish poetry, going as far back to the medieval *Buile Shuibhne*.

Maddern – and the publishers at the always strong Belfast-based Lifeboat Press – have managed a tough feat with *Queering the Green*: pulling together the distinct voices of a variegated community, while placing at the forefront sensuality, not only in the subject matter of the poems themselves, but also through the experience of language and through the immersive experience of offering up such a rich ocean within which readers may swim. As Maddern writes in the introduction: 'Poetry, by its very nature, is a bit other, a bit queer. If we accept that, then every poem is a queering of language.'

Ben Townley-Canning is the editor of fourteen poems, *a London-based magazine dedicated to LGBTQ+ poets.*

FROM THE ARCHIVES

Polina Barskova, Air Raid, *translated by Valzhyna Mort*,
Ugly Duckling Presse, £20, ISBN 9781946433701
Ilya Kaminsky, Dancing in Odessa, *Faber, £8.99*,
ISBN 9780571369188

Sasha Dugdale on tableaux vivants of resistance

. . .

Polina Barskova is a Russian-language poet and scholar who lives in the US. Acclaimed by Russian speakers, she is one of the better-kept secrets of US poetry, but with two new books being published – Valzhyna Mort's translation of *Air Raid* and Catherine Ciepiela's translation of Barskova's essays *Living Pictures* (Pushkin Press) – this is set to change.

The subject of her scholarship and recent poetry is the literature of the Siege of Leningrad. The Nazi besieged Leningrad for nearly three years between 1941 and 1944, killing at least 630,000 and reducing a proud and elegant metropolis to a dying city filled with 'shadow puppets'. And yet, as Barskova makes plain in her conversation with Mort 'in lieu of an afterword' in *Air Raid*, any history of individual suffering was quickly stifled as Leningrad was rebuilt and towering granite monuments erected. An unmentioned mass grave lay under her childhood playground, but the airwaves were filled with heroic symphonies and the drone of military parades. Pathos and grandeur occupied the historical space, and the individual in all her ridiculousness and unhappiness disappeared.

It is not as if there were no individual accounts. The Siege, as Barskova puts it, 'produced verbal diarrhoea', and her scholarly work has been concerned with the archives of diaries, letters, literature and documentary evidence of civilian lives. In *Air Raid*, she takes some of the lives she has researched, reworks the texts they have produced and makes each something uncomfortably alive. This is very far from being documentary: the lyric voice is brutally insightful, grotesque in its intimate handling of subjects. The lives she describes are filled with the vulgar, the cheap and dispensable, the passing fashion and tasteless joke. No one is magnified to heroic. On the contrary, the telescope is turned the other way; everything is small and inconsequential, the language is the scrappy everyday of much-darned underclothes, blackened milk tins and dentures.

'What were they if not converging arteries of memory?' Barskova asks in a lyrical piece in *Living Pictures*. The poems in *Air Raid* are also converging arteries, part of a circulatory system of memory, trying desperately to keep a past alive, despite the brutal and constant lopping away of truth. This is no aesthetic project, not while we witness a war justified by a history of slithering lies and evasions. Returning the blood supply to the past and its victims is a form of civic defiance. And yet sometimes, this chilly lack of sentiment makes the reader squirm. Of the poet Olga Berggolts, who was beaten during an interrogation and miscarried as a result, she writes in 'A Guide to Leningrad Writers, Veterans 1941–1945': 'girl, good luck! / In fact, tough luck: / NKVD man knocks a chair from under you / (a slop of grease)'.

But this anti-sentimental harshness is the essential redress for the Soviet heroic mode. Take the wonderful cycle of poems about Zinaida C., a 'piss-poor' lady translator who disappeared – perhaps her corpse was frozen into a snowdrift. According to a hostile and misogynist review of the damsel translator, her lamentable French translations are 'immensely shallow'. The snippets of this apparently authentic review proceed to disintegrate into a babble of wild grief for the translator, who is a grave, a hole, her mouth sunken and denture-less. Her death, who knows how or where, redeems her from mediocrity because she is at least (at most) human, a reproductive unit: 'mumsy babushka devochka ovary'. Aren't we all Zinaida C., whose main fault, 'reckless negligence when handling foreign property', might be said of anyone who practises translation? But just as sentiment rises in the throat, Barskova kicks us back to sentience: 'how did you, little pimple, break out onto the dragon's back?'

Empathy of the sort practised by Barskova may not be tinged with pathos because it is dynamic and living, and its music is vivid and brutal like an electric shock or a slap in the face. Valzhyna Mort's translation is similarly astringent, but necessarily has a different music. Indifferent to the lip-servicing conventions of Russian translation, Mort seizes the angry polyphony of the poetry and gleefully transforms it into a shocking new English chorus. In place of Polina's defiant rhymes, and her echoes of the short-lived sound poetry of Russian Futurism, Mort deliberately gives us a tacky mix-up, a new language composed of two colonial languages, Russian and English, which she deftly wields like a crowbar in the hands of 'an untraceable Belarusian criminal' as she describes herself to Barskova in their conversation.

The result is a grimly horrifying sound palette with an alertness to 'the pitch that turns a human voice into the voice of a siren' as Mort writes. In the poem 'Auschwitz-Birkenau, a Guided Tour for American Students', the Russian rhyme ropes together jaw and dream, us and gas. Mort drags instead numb, pneuma, gum into line. In English the poem is as wayward as Barskova's account is roundabout, but it has fundamentally the same air of grievous distraction as the original, the same psychological need to riff in the face of wrath.

A very different city lays bare its myths and secrets in Ilya Kaminsky's *Dancing in Odessa*. A Southern city, as warm as Petersburg is chilly and befogged; a city known for theatricality, humour and expansive gestures, as much as wantonness and cruelty. Odessa is brightly-coloured and flower-filled in the wonderful paintings of Yefim Ladyzhensky, alive and kicking in the gangsters of Isaac Babel's *Odessa Stories* – and yet pogroms, the Holocaust and Soviet brutalities cast their long shadows over its avenues. It is this combination of shocking violence and a fragrant Southern over-ripeness and warmth that characterise *Dancing in Odessa*, symbolised visually by the tomato (Kaminsky's motif through two books): red as fresh blood and sweet-rotting in summer markets.

I first read this collection when it was published by Arc in 2014, and it's good to return to it in this new edition after reading *Deaf Republic* (2019), as so many of the shapes in the later and more allegorical work are present here. *Deaf Republic* foreshadows the current and hideous war in Ukraine: as I write Odessa is being shelled by Russians, and occupied Kherson might be the stage for Kaminsky's terrifying theatre of resistance. But for all that Kaminsky is a poet of hopefulness and buoyancy, tenderness, erotic love and attachment to a town and its people, as seen in the poem 'In Praise of Laughter': 'She hung her husband's / Where days bend and straighten / in a city that belongs to no nation / but all the nations of wind.'

Kaminsky's town is an accumulation of fables, in which reality is transfigured by love. He is a born storyteller and raises up the ordinary life, depicting it with a filmmaker's eye, as in the poem 'Aunt Rose': 'She hung her husband's / picture on a wall in her apartment. Each month / on a different wall. I now see her with that picture, hammer / in her left hand, nail in her mouth.'

In his long sequence 'Musica Humana', one of a number of moving poetic tributes to Kaminsky's poetic forebears, he speaks of the poet Osip Mandelstam with the same transfiguring love: the poet's life and art are drawn into a mythic tapestry of eternally occurring events which resist the finality of the poet's violent death. In this sequence lines from Mandelstam are drawn into new association: 'She opened her body, lay on his stomach. / *We will meet in Petersburg*, he said, / *we have buried the sun there.*'

Both Mort and Kaminsky speak of rising above their different linguistic estates in similar terms: all linguistic matter as being a single language (Mort), or as the poet being above all 'a human being' (Kaminsky). As I read both books of poetry, and all three voices, I was minded to think of the way in which the transfer of languages deepens the voice, broadens the current, like a river rushing towards the sea.

Sasha Dugdale is a poet, playwright and translator, most recently of a selection of Maria Stepanova's poetry, War of the Beasts and the Animals *(Bloodaxe, 2021).*

POTENT PERSONIFICATION

Joelle Taylor, C+nto & Othered Poems, *The Westbourne Press,*
£10.99, ISBN 9781908906489

Nathaniel Rosenthalis on erasures, nostalgia and progress

. . .

This 'is a book of silences', opens Joelle Taylor's *C+nto &
Othered Poems, not with a poem but a prose preface. This
preface goes on to tell us that 'the second chapter [of the book] looks
at my personal history and is focused on the loss of my friends, and of
my exile as a consequence of my sexuality.' Taylor points to 'constant
state-endorsed abuse', such as being 'spat at in school, punched in
the back of the head while walking home, attacked on buses, chased
from bars, followed home by whistling men, to name a few. I wear
the abuse as a suit.' This explanation sets us up for sometimes similar
verbal treatments in the poetic portion of the book, where, as one
poem puts it, 'you cut your first suit out of the thick silence when you
enter a room' ('ROUND TWO – the body as protest'). The metaphor
of violence (and its familiar rhyme choice, silence, recalling the AIDS
protest slogan about the two) appears here, with a shift to the second
person and an elaborated image. But the image is essentially the same.
That the book has this kind of thesis-driven, explanatory preface; that

imagery in the preface repeats and recurs in the poems, is a testament to the urgency of Taylor's project. She believes in poems enough to craft them and arrange them with obvious care, but she doesn't want their major messaging and historical context to be lost on any reader.

It is this attentiveness to audience that may explain Taylor's reliance on what some might call a simple poetic device but one that is historically major, and powerful. Streetlamps 'watch a woman pass & text each other' ('Scene One'). History becomes 'a man packing a suitcase / what he leaves behind more valuable // than what is taken' ('Vitrine – vi'). In a bar, '[a] fluorescent strip light undresses & the white tiles watch' ('Scene Four'). Violence 'is a girl / backed up against herself everything about her   ghost   everything   bed.' In 'Summer All Night Long', light becomes a woman with 'poor / impulse control' who:

> throws herself
> at the feet of willow bois
> while summer waits
> by the open door, fans herself
> as bois beg water....

Taylor's book, winner of the 2021 T.S. Eliot Prize, re-draws a map of the erased world of lesbians through many literary manoeuvres, but personification, in my view, is the most surprising and often the most potent one in her hands. It's a canny connection that Taylor's tome won this award, given that Eliot himself was, in addition to being a pivotal proponent of the extended sequence, a major user of the device. Personification turns out to be an ideal response to systemic depersonalisation.

Or that's the claim that comes to me now. It might seem odd that I be tempted to make arguments about literary technique, to focus on the personification of inanimate objects and abstractions. This is, after all, a book that is very much all about justice for women who have been, as the book's preface emphasises, murdered and silenced: butches, bois, studs, stones, femmes, high femmes, bulls, bull dykes, bull daggers, and silverbacks (I quote here from the glossary of slang supplied in the preface – that there is this glossary is another indication of the book's project and its desire to connect to a wide audience). But personification, a frequent device in antiquity through the Middle Ages, seems an indispensable strategy and of a piece with the book's commitment to perceiving and pinpointing the historical dimensions of erasure of lesbians, from the epigraphic definition of cuntare in its latinate, meaning to narrate a story, to the noting of the slang word *invert*, a 'medicalised name for a lesbian, circa 1920s.'

Personification in Taylor's book restores a kind of mythos to lesbians. In fact, one of the poems is called 'Valentine creation myth'. This poem, focused on one of the book's recurring characters, begins as follows:

> it is said she
> built her motorcycle
> from spare washing
> machine parts an
> old Nintendo controller
> & a flick knife
> her brother left
> her

The use of several recurring characters in a book of poems points to a long-standing tradition of allegorical writing as well, wherein poets use elements of storytelling to conjure a reality other than the present one for an audience.

The personifications also reinforce the didactic purpose of Taylor's project. Consider this opening from a section of 'Summer All Night Long':

> two truths can exist in the same space.
> they lean at opposite ends of the bar
> turned away from one another
> watching the others reflection
> in her pint.
> her architecture.
> her present. her unyielding.

Personifying truth as two different lesbians in a bar makes their lives central for the book's audience, an audience made up of lesbians and non-lesbians alike. That Taylor develops this image through these lines, with philosophical attentiveness and imagistic detail in such a vivid way, is one way to teach readers and the overall audience (I use audience and reader interchangeably, as Taylor also performs on stage, in the oral tradition of poetry). And what is the book trying to teach? This is a book that wears a certain nostalgia knowingly. From the preface: 'While this book is set in what is now thought of as the "golden age of the gay", we have regressed as a community.' The lesson, then, is about progression. This clear claim set me up to expect a brittle poetry of reducible claims; however, in part through manoeuvres like the personifications, the poems echo forcibly for me, sometimes on a level comparable to the horrifying statistics in the preface.

Lest it seem that personification is the only modus operandi of this book, it's worth pointing out Taylor's other dominant mood of classic, or at least familiar, metaphor. For example, the face is a mask: 'strangers take their faces off when I enter rooms' ('The Unbelong'). A body is an article of clothing: 'I was a girl who had grabbed her body / from the wrong coat hook' ('Homosapien'). A few times, a body is a room: 'A small girl walks into her body / & turns the bedroom light on' ('The Unbelong') and 'at the centre of every boi / is a bare room / & inside a swinging lightbulb' ('Angel'). A body is also placed: 'your body a foreign country' ('ROUND ONE – the body as battleground'). Rifle through any number of contemporary poetry publications and doubtless similar metaphors will emerge, and matter. The force of this book is rather the arc of the whole, which, moving from prose poem to tidy couplets to scripted scenes with stage and lighting and sound directions, is decidedly inventive in its rich conjurings.

Nathaniel Rosenthalis is a poet, actor and critic, and the author of the pamphlet, 24 Hour Air *(PANK, 2022).*

SHADOWS

Denise Riley, Lurex, *Picador*, £10.99, ISBN 9781529078138
Lucy Mercer, Emblem, *Prototype*, £12.00, ISBN 9781913513221

Edwina Attlee on lure, the lyric fragment and liberated ekphrasis

. . .

Lurex is a type of yarn that shimmers. It is made from synthetic film and vaporised aluminium, silver or gold. Wikipedia tells us the Lurex company started production in England in the 1970s. The name was based on the English lure, for temptation and attractiveness. The question of attraction, people coming together and breaking apart, being longed for and longing for, one's own attractiveness and attraction's absence are all thought about in Denise Riley's *Lurex*, the poet's most recent collection following *Say Something Back* (2016). The collection is formally and thematically more various, full of jokes, prose poems, long poems and tiny lyric fragments. The struggle to live alone is related wittily, pithily and ultimately with heart-breaking economy:

Be quick

I've no companion
bar a shadow
pointing backwards.

Dear life, don't ghost me yet!
Find me a home
Through stumbling rain.

The 'shadow / pointing backwards' threads its 'dark yet sparkly' ('Lurex') fingers through the collection, and from the vantage point of a life lived, past attractions are tied to childhood and adulthood traumas:

'You knew how to pick 'em, all right,' tease the friends who aren't alone.
I never 'picked' anyone – felt lucky to get auditioned, or even viewed.
Am I, thanks to that feeling, a source of darkness my best efforts prolong.
('Another Agony in the Garden')

Lurex is also part of a specific cultural history, closely related to darkness; it's part of the democratisation of *sparkling*. I imagine girls getting ready for dances, applying makeup, lining up to look in the mirror, turning this way and that to see the light pick out the metal in the thread. Carolyn Steedman writes about how working-class women, in contrast with their male contemporaries, were 'without class, because the cut and fall of a skirt and good leather shoes can take you across the river and to the other side: the fairy-tales tell you that goose-girls may marry kings' ('Landscape for a Good Woman'). In 'How some things once came', Riley describes a series of potentially magical objects, 'Quant catalogues', 'tights', 'Sobranies'; each suggestive of a hopeful youth, passwords to a fairy-tale of their own. Riley makes each object simultaneously immediate and frail, 'Quant catalogues came sketched on tracing paper.' The fairy-tale is shown to be just that, and the poem lodges instead in the political reality of the 1970s, amid the campaign for abortion law reform and the experience of single motherhood; 'Forms to prove they'd qualify for free school meals came on blurry lined paper.' The speaker is the recipient of these written forms of instruction and permission, they exist between these unutterably different forces which govern both action and possibility; on the one hand, fashion and consumption, on the other state sanctioned custody and benefits.

Helen Charman has made an argument for a continued critical attention to be paid towards the radical political context for Riley's writing ('Where do I put Myself if Public Life's Destroyed?', *The White Review*) but a poem like this makes it seem a simple task. The received category of 'a woman' is sketched, felt, rejected and spoken from simultaneously. Riley populates her collection, which can be read as extravagantly literary, speaking back to Burns, Pope, Saba and Notley, with objects from a distinctly feminist history. Her poetry threads these things into the existing narratives and they are richer for her stitching.

> In the kitchen at home, iron pails held sheep's heads being steeped to make Scotch broth. Other pails of cold water came and went every few weeks. Those were to soak the white cloths, seeping out their clouds of blood.
>
> ('Facts of the 1950s')

The final sparkle that lines these poems is Riley's use of metre, a fact she goads the critic about in 'Tick tock'. The many ears in the book listen once and twice and, so the speaker of this poem tells us, cadence itself has an ear that 'lip-reads – // so "sense must seem an echo to the sound"' ('Tick tock').

It is hard not to think that Riley must be an influence on Lucy Mercer whose first collection *Emblem* is grounded, at least in part, in experiences of pregnancy and early motherhood, and which takes up the form, perfected by Riley, of the lyric fragment. It is worth noting that both collections have explanatory and enlivening notes which undo nothing of the poem's magic but rather send you back through the book and out (of course) to search for further information online. Mercer has written about the book being *from* rather than *about* motherhood and what can be deduced about that location is its pliant nature, the sense that what is known can slip, that certainties no longer apply.

Mercer presses upon language in such a way as to make it shimmer, or blink, or stagger. Her use of repetition is wonderfully particular and strange:

> so, you think
> so so
> so, a word said by no-one

and the moon rises
and so   again
so
and so

there seems
a distant country
sleeping all alone
for you
to know

('Ten Shifts')

Motherhood is also a shrinking of the frame of reference, a tactic Mercer has applied doubly as the result of an encounter with a book of emblems, a peculiar form of illustrated epigram semi-invented by the fifteenth-century jurist and philologist Andrea Alciato. The book reproduces some 400-year-old images from the 1621 version of his *Emblematum liber*. By focusing intently on these sources, and by being curtailed in other ways by the frame of motherhood, the poems accrue an intensity that is reminiscent of Gaston Bachelard's sense of the miniature. Discussing the botanical descriptions in an encyclopedia of herbs, he writes, 'Large issues from small [...] thanks to a liberation from all obligations of dimensions, a liberation that is a special characteristic of the activity of the imagination' (*The Poetics of Space*).

Minute details of observation, coupled with a phenomenological faithfulness to the experience of not being sure, of working something out, lead to a special kind of alchemy, and it does feel liberated; I do not think the result can be called ekphrastic in the normal sense. The texts are little see-saws of sense, tipping one way and then another in a fitting tribute to her source. In the opening poem 'Emblem' we get to see the poet really handling her words, enjoying as it were their feel in her mouth, the sticky and sumptuous pleasure of describing something as being like 'the gizzard of a turkey', or 'the near-fluorescent fractals of a complicated Romanesco broccoli'. The mouthfuls become metaphorical, a book becomes a poem, a poem becomes an embryo, 'this lumpy ball / thrown into the future'. And then the speaker is looking at an image again and the poem seems to pivot between image and text, *looking* in writing, and getting lost in its looking; 'while all around a border of tortuous scrollwork brings the inside/ to the outside, this folly, fol-de-rol – *festina lente*'. It's an enormously satisfying collection, each poem singing on its own and speaking to the others as they go.

> Opened a door onto a drawn field full of tigers that were licking
> the light, but all I could think at that moment while watching them
>   so orange and true was
> I should like to be a drawn field ... with the sun's first joy coming
>   towards me
> holding my mind like a thin blue plastic kite before it's given up to
> the wind, the deep spine resting between beams of light. 'Thalassa we
> see you!' says the light. 'Making all the rivers so salty they cry out
>   in books!'
>
>   ('Shadow')

> *Edwina Attlee is the author of* the cream *(Clinic, 2016),* Roasting Baby
> *(if a leaf falls press, 2016) and* Strayed Homes: Cultural Histories of
> the Domestic in Public *(Bloomsbury, 2021).*

WAR AND PEACE

Carl Phillips, Then the War: Selected Poems 2007–2020,
Carcanet, £14.99, ISBN 9781800172296

Carol Rumens on forgiveness, tenderness and rescue

• • •

This most organic of poetry collections, *Then the War*, is a forest-like network of linguistic relationships. Unusually structured, it begins with an entire new collection, whose title, *Then the War*, provides the umbrella title of the whole volume. A modestly slim representation of six earlier full-length collections follows in chronological order, culminating in the complete text of the chapbook, *Star Map with Action Figures*. Fifteen years' work, an expanse which could have produced variety to the point of dissonance, is instead a homogeneous one-movement symphony. Phillips described himself in an interview with *The Kenyon Review* as 'one of those poets who pushes more deep at something with each book.' The possible mishap of writing the same poem twice doesn't arise: ideas are turned over at different angles and that way gather complexity and momentum. Planned reappearances, as when a line becomes another poem's title, and recurrent images and themes keep the pattern tight.

Part One of the title-collection enables us to learn more of the poet's background through a fine set of autobiographical lyric essays 'Among the Trees'. The most significant tree is a fig-tree growing in the yard of the poet's childhood house in Portland, Oregon. In a traumatic adventure that would become his earliest memory, he climbed the tree as his parents called him indoors: 'it seemed like a game'. He lost his footing, fell, but was caught by a branch on the way down, saved but suspended helplessly by the underpants. His mother wanted to fetch a ladder, but his African-American father said he should be left to hang in the tree for a while to learn obedience. The narrative, unfolded till now with Phillips's usual slow elegance and restraint, takes on a new terseness: scathingly, he notes his father's lack of 'attention to historical resonance in our daily lives' and 'can't help thinking about the place of trees in African-American history, as the site for lynching.' The young child is left hanging in the tree as night falls. Phillips closes the memoir by asking 'Who can say how related this is to my refusal, all my life, to believe forgiveness exists?' Forgiveness, tenderness and rescue are among the ethical values the whole collection repeatedly interrogates.

Trees, leaves, horses, dogs, swans, bees, the sea, snow, light, the wind: these are among the recurring emblems of Phillips's physical landscape. The reader never doubts either that Phillips has observed them and all their subtle changes in real life (the effects of wind on water, for instance, are noted in detail) nor that these elements stand in metaphorical relationship with the human and the moral. The symbolic treatment of pastoral provides disguise and liberation, and ways to explore the questions of domination and vulnerability engendered by sex. There's a tactful and truth-seeking close reading, in a majority of the poems, of queer relationships and social power dynamics, but the view of the drama is a distant one, of 'emotion recollected in tranquillity' – though with no trace of Wordsworthian complacency. It's expansive enough to become a reading of the basic rates and high interest of much of human exchange.

In the title poem, the war is remarkably stylised. Earlier, the protagonists have made a safe, pleasant and sufficiently expansive space for themselves ('hawk's nest, winter-nest, stamina as a form of faith, little / cove that a life equals'), but they are taken by surprise. The ominous three-word statement, 'Then the war', has a line to itself. The war is presented as ritualistic: 'Then the field, and the mounted police / parading their proud-looking horses across it.' Order is restored next morning, and the couple seem at peace. 'They closed their eyes. / If gently, hard to say *how* gently. / Then the war was nothing that still bewildered them, if it ever had.' The image of 'mounted police' suggests state-endorsed violence, and it's uncertain whether this violence includes the conduct of the relationship. If so, it has been pacified and absorbed. But in a book called *Then the War* the war-making must be a continuous present-tense with a reach into the future. It's one of the activities the animal-body does with another animal-body; it's what the mind echoes in its own argument with itself and society.

The Phillips poem is almost invariably the demonstration of a thought process. In the long, discursive epilogue of the title-collection, there's a moment when the narrator considers his move from a seaside residence to a location some distance from the sea. He remembers the pioneers and the 'teetered wagons that they / called prairie schooners out of / sheer nostalgia, already missing / the sea'. This prompts a characteristically scrupulous question-to-self:

> *Is* that nostalgia? Or is it
> more like what Xenophanes says,
> how if cows could draw, the gods
> in their pictures would have
> horns, the gods of birds
> would have feathers everywhere,
> each would brandish, for
> stateliness, two wings for mastering
> a wind strong enough to bring
> the stars down, as we used to say, before
> to touch meant collision, back
> when sex was what mattered
>   most; seemed to.
>
> ('This Far In')

The suggestion that the sea might be god for an originally aquatic creature, man, is compellingly illustrated, but it's only a passing thought. Erotic meditation resurfaces some lines later, with the assertion that sex 'still matters' and a sudden, shy swerve into third-person narration:

         let sex be governed
by that same restraint from
any harm unasked for. It almost
sounds like prayer sometimes,
       he said, describing light on water.
He said it like the sort of thing,
after sex, one simply says. Entering
the body, pulling gently back
out of it – is that so little for a life
to have come to?

It's not all the life has come to, we will discover, reading on, sharing the poet's reluctance for closure: 'Let's see what happens' is what the wind says to him finally. The quoted passages are powerful because of the balance of scepticism and idealism, emotional turbulence and thoughtful imperturbability.

There is a didactic quality in Phillips, but it's more inner- than outer-directed, and gains from a classicist's coolly historical frame of reference. Self-help sometimes overlaps with contemporary poetry, and there are many dangers, from banality to portentousness, for poets offering their own 'journey' as life-guide. Phillips operates in an altogether superior league. He lets us learn by watching the teacher teach himself, by hearing him think aloud. The illumination can be enthralling and all-enveloping, as when, in 'Civilisation', he picks up the refrain 'there's an art to everything' for the final time:

       There's an art
   to everything. Even
   turning away. How

eventually even hunger
   can become a space
to live in. How they made
   out of shamelessness something
   beautiful, for as long as they could.

Carol Rumens' latest collection is The Mixed Urn *(Sheep Meadow, 2019).*

AN EXPERT WEAVER

Olive Senior, Hurricane Watch: New and Collected Poems,
Carcanet, £25.00, ISBN 9781800172166

Zakia Carpenter-Hall on a Jamaican poet and Walt Whitman

. . .

When I lived in Detroit, I had a friend who founded a collective called Red Thread Theatre. She led a small group of people to each select an event in their lives and develop those into theatre pieces, which they later performed jointly for a live audience. There wouldn't be a specific theme selected; the founder knew that at some level all human experience and life is interconnected, which was how the company got its name. 'Red Thread' came from the East Asian concept 'The Red Thread of Fate', believed to link soulmates. When reading Olive Senior's *Hurricane Watch: New and Collected Poems*, I re-encountered the concepts of thread as life-line – 'The fibres of belonging to this world' ('Ode to Pablo Neruda') – and artist as weaver. Senior, who is the Poet Laureate of Jamaica, stretches her string beyond lovers to create a web of humanity, nature, divinity, history and more:

The thread that's a red, red line through history
that loops and curls and knots like a net

of discovery, entrapping pirates, bankers and
cutlass blades, planters whips and sinews
of slaves, politicians' lying tongues and the
rachet knife cutting the root of innocence,
the bullet's trajectory riding on collusion:
richman, poorman, beggarman, thief,
policeman, businessman, presidents and those
that preach. If any pass through thread's weave
as knots work loose, the thread will be dragged
by the needle of truth.

('The Eye of Everything')

It's as if the sewing needle's eye is an eye of the world, and nothing escapes its threading. As alluded to in the previous quote, the scale and scope of Senior's subject matter is remarkable. One way that she demonstrates her expertise is through bringing disparate themes together convincingly: drawing hurricanes into relationship with thread; the blowing of a conch shell and the whirlwind of weather; enslaved peoples and the crops they were forced to produce; extraction, imperialism and collected possessions; fables of multiculturalism and biodiversity; nature, the personal and the cosmic. Senior's themes and writing are porous, like Walt Whitman's, allowing for overlap and intersection. She also takes inspiration from Pablo Neruda imploring his reader to '[grasp] poetry like a thread' and adds her own interpretation:

Here's how I see it: This thread is one that crosses your path
like the spider's web. You walk through unaware
The Great Spider still clings to it. So now Spider clings
to you, my friend. This is not an accident. You have been
chosen Spider's apprentice. To master language. As
Trickster, to spin and weave tales. To prophesy and heal.
The go-between serving earth and sky. Sometimes the
messenger left dangling.

After you have taken the thread – the thread you cannot refuse
– you must choose how to handle it.

('Ode to Pablo Neruda')

She manages to do this weaving with candour and nuance. Her poems often have an allegorical feel to them (that is, she writes about the more obvious subject matter in the poem and beyond it).

The aims of Senior's and Whitman's poetic projects appear to be similar: bring multiple peoples, cultures, practices into a bustling collective. However, where Whitman tended to at best gloss over differences and at worst perpetuate the bigotry of his time, Senior's collection tells not only of harmonies but of discord. To continue the thread metaphor, she reveals the underlying tensions along the string. And she's not afraid of this thread of connection breaking or wearing down; in fact, she welcomes it. The thread can be restored:

> So I'm seeking that old woman, the wizard of the cords
> who used to tie up the wind with three knots in a bundle
> and sell it to sailors: 'Mark well, my good man. Loosen
> this knot for light breezes, this one to send you clipping
> along and this – woe betide – for a battering.'
>
> Yes, I let loose the hurricane. And I'm sorry about the
> damage but I forgot which knot was which – that's the
> problem with raw thread it – all looks the same. But my
> hurricane heart feels better for its roaring, for scouring
> the world. For it's the strong wind that cleanses, that
> unburdens and purifies. It uplifted the fallen. And broke
> the thread. But I'll mend it and restring with fresh beads.
>
> ('Ode to Pablo Neruda')

Hers is a poetics of fragmentation and cohesion, of discord and harmonising, of unravelling and knotting, twisting, entangling and tying together:

> I'll make part of this rosary of the Alpha and Omega
> which could serve as the necklace for Brahma
> for Buddha Muhammed the Virgin Mary for Oya.
>
> ('Ode to Pablo Neruda')

At the centre of it all, the root and base of her work are these cosmic, elemental, primal forces and the efforts of an expert weaver.

Life-lines can also uncurl like the breeze and coiled wind at the centre of a conch shell whose shape produces, not oceanic sounds, but an amplification of the surrounding ambient noise. The shell's sound reflects its environment, like the poet reflects hers, an amplifier of worlds:

> What if one day you accidentally
> picked up the right shell – such as I; placed it
>
> to your ear, pressed – by chance – the right
> knob, there would pour out not the croak
> of song soaked-up in sea-water and salt
>
> but the real thing, a blast-out, everybody's
> history: *areito, canto histórico*, a full
> genealogy of this beach, this island people.
>
> ('Shell Blow')

In this persona poem, the speaker is the shell. And truth has an unravelling and stripping down effect wherever it is unleashed, like the hurricane. 'For it's the strong wind that cleanses' ('Ode to Pablo Neruda').

At the beginning of a section titled 'Over the Roofs of the World (2005)', Senior quotes Whitman: 'I too am not a bit tamed, I too am untranslatable, I sound my barbaric yawp over the roofs of the world'. But in some key aspects, Senior's project of interlacing and singing the cycle of life is larger than Whitman's engagement with the gossamer thread. For one, her collected works is physically larger than Whitman's *Leaves of Grass* (1855 edition). *Hurricane Watch* is almost 500 pages, but her work also feels larger in scope in that it includes perspectives that Whitman, regardless of his efforts or vision, couldn't adequately grasp or realise in his poems:

> Friend,
> you do not understand
> sickle cell anaemia

or sleeping on pavements
as we cannot understand
Baseball Season
or Fall

We do not need
interstellar leaps
we want to shorten
distances between
hospitals

And though flies
might cover the fish
in our open marketplaces
that does not kill,
like napalm.

('Letter From the Lesser World')

Not only is Senior aware of what it means to be on the receiving end of Western imperialism, she offers fresh critique and perspective from that vantage point. Senior's poetic expertise and heritage of belonging to multiple cultures with different worldviews and mythologies gives her an increased versatility and sense of how these varying threads, songs, narratives can be woven together. After all, she has had to weave together the complex threads and fragments of her own life and histories:

Listen child, said my father
from the quicksand of his life:
Study rivers. Learn everything.
Rivers may find beginnings
in the clefts of separate mountains
Yet all find their true homes
in the salt of one sea.

('Cockpit Country Dreams')

Though Neruda and Whitman are among Senior's literary predecessors, she is the gifted protégée, both stripping back and building up threads of human experience and relationality to the non-human world. Like a red thread of interrelationship, her poems reinforce a sense of Earth as a cohabitational space, an intricate system of networks, roots and unexpected connections. Current and historic tensions, breaks in our delicate system of life-lines, affect us all. Senior's threads compellingly trace links between our global environmental crisis and the colonialist agenda to subdue, extract and possess. Perhaps this is why Senior's poetry so clearly emphasises the necessity of remaking and demonstrates an understanding that even deeply ingrained origin stories can be unravelled and retold to reveal some of the invisible root systems below.

Zakia Carpenter-Hall is a PhD candidate at Royal Holloway University of London researching Black feminist poetics, Walt Whitman and how poetic traditions expand.

THE GEOFFREY DEARMER
PRIZE 2021

Judge: CAConrad

The economy of Samatar Elmi's poem 'The Snails' was immediately striking, using only the words necessary to resonate inside us long after reading. In trusting us to understand with minimal language, it is clear he knows the reader's creativity is as important as his own. It is beautiful not to have a poem overwritten for lack of trusting the audience. The space around the poem offers ample opportunity for our imaginations to connect all the corresponding ideas Elmi provides. While I admire the poem's construction, the information feeding our minds in 'The Snails' makes this a hinge poem, or rather, a poem turning inside us so we will never forget reading and grappling with it. Samatar Elmi's conflation of a snail carrying its home on its back with the lives of those living in exile is riveting; their 'songs and laments resound', and we pause to listen intently, with purpose and reverence.

As someone who reads poetry every day, I am happy to find a poem that stamps itself to my heart in archival ink. A poem so good I ache for it to expand or multiply into a collection. Go ahead and Google 'snails are...' as the poet suggests, for this is one of those times we want to build a world around the poet's words. The annoying computer document I am writing this into is warning me that I have used the words 'poet' and 'poem' too many times... poem, poet, poem, poet, you are wrong, computer, not too many times. It was an honour to judge this contest. Choosing one poem was difficult, for there were many brilliant poems. 'The Snails' caught me with a gasp on the first reading, and the sensation remains the same with each new reading. My very best to Samatar Elmi.

CAConrad is the author of almost a dozen books, including AMANDA PARADISE: Resurrect Extinct Vibration (Wave, 2021) and While Standing in Line for Death (Wave, 2017), winner of the 2018 Lambda Literary Award for Gay Poetry. They have also received a Creative Capital Award and a Pew Fellowship, among other honours. They teach at Columbia University and the Sandberg Art Institute.

SAMATAR ELMI

The Snails

I mean, the analogy writes itself
like the onion in a grand conceit
though we really are like two slugs
in a derelict mausoleum.
Google 'snails are...'
Dangerous. Slow.
Destroying my garden.
Our jobs and our women.
You, who cannot speak snail,
wouldn't understand how the shell
was the gift and curse of diaspora,
how our songs and laments resound
in our half-remembered houses
that we carry to forget, to carry on.

Samatar Elmi *is a poet, PhD candidate and educator. His writing plays in the liminal spaces between racial, socio-cultural and political identity claims. He has been shortlisted for the Venture Award, the Complete Works II, New Generation African Poets and is a graduate of the Young Inscribe Mentoring Programme. His poems have appeared in* Magma, Iota, Ink Sweat and Tears, Myths of the Near Future, Scarf, The Echoing Gallery *and* The Cadaverine.

The Geoffrey Dearmer Prize is awarded annually to the best poem in *The Poetry Review* by a poet who had not, at the time their work appeared, published a full collection. It is funded through the generosity of the Dearmer family in honour of poet and Poetry Society member Geoffrey Dearmer.

CONTRIBUTORS

Gbenga Adesina is a Nigerian poet and essayist. He was the 2019–20 Olive B. O'Connor Poetry Fellow at Colgate University • **Rae Armantrout** has published numerous poetry collections, including *Versed* (Wesleyan University Press, 2010), which won the Pulitzer Prize. Her most recent book is *Finalists* (2021) • **Jakky Bankong-Obi** is based in Abuja, Nigeria. Her chapbook *What Still Yields* was chosen for publication in the New-Generation African Poets box set (Akashic and APBF, 2022) • **Gray Behagg** is a non-binary poet and nurse based in Brighton. Their work has appeared in *Ambit, Magma, The Emma Press Anthology of Love* and *The Rialto*. They won the 2013 Bridport Prize for poetry • **Chad Bennett** is author of *Your New Feeling Is the Artifact of a Bygone Era* (Sarabande Books, 2020). He teaches poetry and poetics at the University of Texas at Austin • **Meron Berhanu** is a poet and short-story writer from Kilburn, London. Her work has been published in *The Black Anthology* (10:10 Press, 2021) and *22 Under 22 Anthology* (Flexible Press, 2020) • **Joshua Blackman** is a poet and photographer from Bognor Regis. His poems have appeared in *Ambit, The Moth Magazine* and *The White Review* • **Kevin Breathnach** is author of *Tunnel Vision* (Faber, 2019) and *Morphing* (The Lifeboat, 2020) • **Kimberly Campanello** is associate professor of Creative Writing in the School of English at the University of Leeds • **Laura Elliott's** most recent publications include *this is hunting* (Distance No Object, 2019), *rib-boning* (Moot Press, 2019) and *lemon, egg, bread* (Test Centre, 2017) • **Jameson Fitzpatrick** is the author of *Pricks in the Tapestry* (Birds, LLC, 2020), a finalist for the 2021 Thom Gunn Award, and a clinical associate professor of expository writing at New York University • **Oakley Flanagan** is a writer, poet and playwright • **Peter Gizzi's** recent books include *Now It's Dark* (Wesleyan, 2020), *Sky Burial: New and Selected Poems* (Carcanet, 2020) and *Archeophonics* (Wesleyan, 2016) • **Garth Greenwell** is the author of *What Belongs to You* and *Cleanness*. He lives in Iowa City • **Bonnie Hancell** is a Queer, Trans creative from Northern England • **Selima Hill** is author of *Men Who Feed Pigeons* (Bloodaxe, 2021), shortlisted for the T.S. Eliot Prize, Forward Prize and Rathbones Folio Prize • **Safiya Kamaria Kinshasa** is a British-born Barbadian-raised poet who chiefly uses movement to inform her practice • **Karl Knights'** prose and poetry have appeared in *The Guardian, The Dark Horse* and *Poetry London*. He won the New Poets Prize 2021 and has recently published his debut pamphlet, *Kin* (The Poetry Business, 2022) • **Noelle Kocot** is an American poet. She is the author of nine full-length collections of poetry, and her latest, *Ascent of the Mothers*, is forthcoming (Wave Books, 2023) • **Timothy Liu's** latest book is *Luminous Debris: New & Selected Legerdemain 1992–2017* (Barrow Street Press, 2018), he lives in Manhattan and Woodstock, N.Y. • **Fran Lock** is the author of numerous chapbooks and poetry collections, most recently *Hyena! Jackal! Dog!* (Pamenar Press, 2021) • **Hannah Lowe's** *The Kids* won the Costa Book of the Year, 2021 • **Katy Mack's** work has appeared in *Ambit, Poetry International, Poetry Birmingham Literary Journal* and various other publications • **Chris McCabe's** work spans art forms and genres including poetry, fiction, non-fiction, drama and visual art; the poems published here will appear in his next collection with Penned in the Margins in 2023 • **Maureen N. McLane's** next book, *What You Want: Poems*, will be out in

2023 • **Dante Micheaux** is the author of *Circus* (Indolent Books, 2018), which won the *Four Quartets* Prize from the Poetry Society of America and the T.S. Eliot Foundation, and *Amorous Shepherd* (Sheep Meadow Press, 2010) • **Geraldine Monk's** poetry was first published in the 1970s. Her most recent collection of poems, *They Who Saw the Deep* (Free Verse Editions/ Parlor Press), was published in 2016. She lives in Sheffield • **Luis Muñoz** is the author of seven books of poems and his awards include the Ciudad de Córdoba, Generación del 27 and Ojo Crítico prizes • **Miguel Murphy** is author of *Shoreditch*, and two previous collections of poetry. He lives in Southern California, where he is on faculty at Santa Monica College • **Daljit Nagra's** next collection, *indiom*, will be published by Faber in 2023 • **Idra Novey** is the author of the novels *Those Who Knew* and *Ways to Disappear* and several books of poems • **Sandeep Parmar** is professor of English literature at the University of Liverpool. Her third collection, *Faust*, will be published by Shearsman in 2022 • **Lara Pawson** is a writer living in London. She is the author of two books and is currently working on a third inspired by objects • **J.H. Prynne** is a prolific poet. His collections include *The White Stones* (1969), *The Oval Window* (1983) and *Poems* (Bloodaxe, 2015, 3rd Edition) • **Sam Riviere** is the author of *81 Austerities* (Faber, 2012), *Kim Kardashian's Marriage* (Faber, 2015) and *After Fame* (Faber, 2020). He lives in Edinburgh, where he runs the micropublisher If a Leaf Falls Press • **Gemma Robinson** is a senior lecturer in English Studies at the University of Stirling, having previously held lectureships at Newcastle University and Trinity College Dublin • **Fortunato Salazar** is a writer and translator who lives in West Hollywood, California • **Iliassa Sequin** (1940–2019) was born in Greece and lived for many years in East London; her *Collected Complete Poems* (Grey Suit Editions) was published in 2021 • **Xiao Yue Shan** is a poet born in Dongying, China who now lives on Vancouver Island. A chapbook, *How Often I Have Chosen Love*, was published in 2019. A full-length collection, *Then Telling Be the Antidote*, is forthcoming in 2022. • **Andy Spragg** has published a number of books of poetry, most recently *O Buster* (RunAmok, 2021). He lives in London • **Carol Watts'** most recent collection, *Kelptown* (Shearsman, 2020), explores the coastal landscape where the south downs meet the sea as an imaginary zone of inundation and interspecies dependence. She is a professor of literature and poetics at the University of Sussex • **Alice White**, originally from Kansas, lives in rural France. A graduate of the University of St Andrews, she is a recipient of the Langston Hughes Award and is a two-time Bread Loaf Rona Jaffe Foundation Scholar. Her poetry has recently appeared in *The Threepenny Review* and *The Cortland Review* • **Jay Whittaker** lives in Edinburgh. She has published two poetry collections, *Sweet Anaesthetist* (2020) and *Wristwatch*, which was awarded Scottish Poetry Book of 2018 in the Saltire Society Literary Awards • **Mark Wunderlich** is the author of four books of poetry. He lives in New York's Hudson Valley.

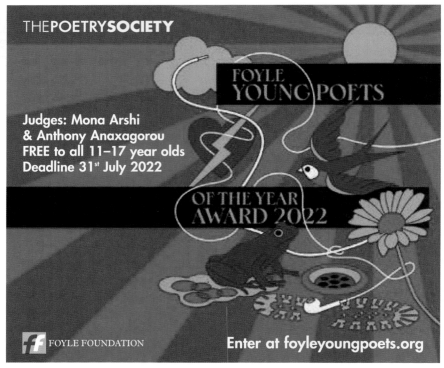